1000 THINGS
YOU SHOULD KNOW ABOUT

WILD ANIMALS

WILD
ANIMALS

John Farndon

PUBLISHING

**This edition first published in 2003 for
Books are Fun**

First published in 2000 by
Miles Kelly Publishing,
Bardfield Centre, Great Bardfield, Essex, CM7 4SL, U.K.
Copyright © Miles Kelly Publishing 2000, 2003

2 4 6 8 10 9 7 5 3 1

Library of Congress Cataloging-in-Publication Data on file
at the Library of Congress

ISBN 1-902947-32-0

Editorial Director: Anne Marshall
Editors: Amanda Learmonth, Jenni Rainford
Assistant: Liberty Newton
Americanization: Cindy Leaney
Written and designed by: John Farndon and Angela Koo

Printed in China

CONTENTS

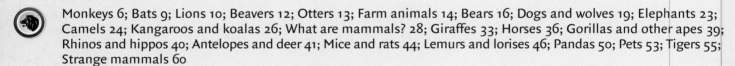
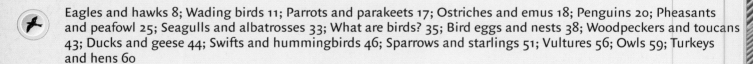
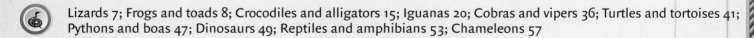
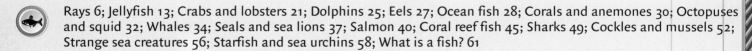
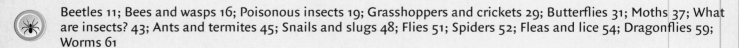
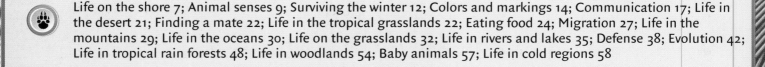

KEY

 Mammals

 Birds

 Reptiles and amphibians

 Sea creatures

 Insects, spiders, and creepy crawlies

 How animals live

Monkeys

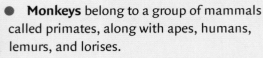

- **Monkeys** belong to a group of mammals called primates, along with apes, humans, lemurs, and lorises.

- **Monkeys** live mostly in trees, and their hands have fingers and their feet have toes for gripping branches. Most monkeys also have tails.

- **There are 150** species of monkey, and they live in tropical forests in Asia, Africa, and the Americas.

- **New World monkeys** (from the Americas) live in trees and often have muscular tails that can grip like a hand. These tails are described as prehensile.

◄ *Baboons such as the Hamadryas (sacred) baboon are large, dog-like monkeys which are well adapted to living on the ground in African bush country.*

- **New World monkeys** include howler monkeys, spider monkeys, woolly monkeys, and capuchins, as well as marmosets, and tamarins such as the golden lion tamarin.

- **Old World monkeys** (from Africa and Asia) live on grasslands as well as in forests. They include baboons, colobus monkeys, langurs, and macaques.

- **Old World monkeys** do not have a prehensile tail, but their thumbs and fingers can point together, like ours can, so they can grasp things well.

- **The proboscis monkey** gets its name from its huge nose (proboscis is another word for nose).

- **Most monkeys** eat anything from fruit to birds' eggs, but baboons may also catch and eat baby antelopes.

> ★ STAR FACT ★
> Howler monkeys can howl so loud that a pair of them can be heard over 3km (2mi) away.

Rays

- **Rays** are a huge group of over 300 species of fish, which includes skates, stingrays, electric rays, manta rays, eagle rays, and guitar fish.

- **Many rays** have flat, almost diamond-shaped bodies, with pectoral fins elongated into broad wings. Guitar fish have longer, more shark-like bodies.

- **A ray's gills** are slot-like openings beneath its fins.

- **Rays have no bones.** Instead, like sharks, they are cartilaginous fish—their body framework is made of rubbery cartilage (you have this in your nose and ears).

- **Rays live mostly** on the ocean floor, feeding on seabed creatures such as oysters, clams, and other shellfish.

- **Manta rays** live near the surface and feed on plankton.

- **The Atlantic manta ray** is the biggest ray, often over 23ft (7m) wide and 20ft (6m) long.

- **Stingrays** get their name from their whip-like tail with its poisonous barbs. A sting from a stingray can make humans very sick.

▲ *Manta rays often bask near the surface of the oceans, with the tips of their pectoral fins poking out of the water.*

- **Electric rays** are tropical rays able to give off a powerful electric charge to defend themselves against attackers.

- **The black torpedo ray** can put out a 220 volt shock, twice as much as a household electric socket.

Lizards

- **Lizards** are a group of 3,800 scaly-skinned reptiles, varying from an inch or so long to the 10ft (3m) long Komodo dragon.

- **Lizards cannot** control their own body heat, and so rely on sunshine for warmth. This is why they live in warm climates and bask in the sun for hours each day.

- **Lizards move** in many ways—running, scampering, and slithering. Some can glide. Unlike mammals, their limbs stick out sideways rather than downward.

- **Most lizards** lay eggs, although a few give birth to live young. But unlike birds or mammals, a mother lizard does not nurture (look after) her young.

- **Most lizards** are meat-eaters, feeding on insects and other small creatures.

> ★ **STAR FACT** ★
> The six-lined race runner lizard of the U.S. southeast can run at 18mph (29km/h).

- **The glass lizard** has no legs. Its tail may break off and lie wriggling as a decoy if it is attacked. It later grows another one.

- **The Australian frilled lizard** has a ruff around its neck. To scare attackers, it can spread out its ruff to make itself look three or four times bigger.

- **Horned lizards** can squirt a jet of blood from their eyes almost as far as 3ft (1m) to repel attackers.

- **The Komodo dragon** of Sumatra is the biggest lizard, weighing 330lb (150kg) or more. It can catch deer and pigs and swallow them whole.

▶ Lizards have four legs and a long tail. In most lizards, the back legs are much stronger than the front, and are used to drive the animal forward in a kind of writhing motion.

Life on the shore

- **Shores** contain a huge variety of creatures which can adapt to the constant change from wet to dry as the tide rolls in and out.

- **Crabs, shellfish,** and other creatures of rocky shores have tough shells to protect them from pounding waves and the sun's drying heat.

- **Anemones, starfish,** and shellfish such as barnacles have powerful suckers for holding on to rocks.

- **Limpets** are the best rock clingers and can only be pried off if caught by surprise.

- **Anemones** may live on a hermit crab's shell, feeding on its leftovers but protecting it with their stinging tentacles.

▲ Crabs, lugworms, sandhoppers, shellfish, and many other creatures live on shores. Many birds come to feed on them.

- **Rock pools** are water left behind among the rocks as the tide goes out. They get very warm and salty.

- **Rock pool creatures** include shrimps, hermit crabs, anemones, and fish such as blennies and gobies.

- **Sandy shores** are home to burrowing creatures such as crabs, razor clams, lugworms, sea cucumbers, and burrowing anemones.

- **Sandhoppers** are tiny shelled creatures that live along the tide line, feeding on seaweed.

- **Beadlet anemones** look like blobs of jello on rocks when the tide is out. But when the water returns, they open a ring of flower-like tentacles to feed.

Eagles and hawks

▲ *The bald eagle eats fish, snatching them from rivers.*

- **Eagles and hawks** are among 280 species of raptor (bird of prey). The group also includes kestrels, falcons, goshawks, buzzards, and vultures.

- **Most birds of prey are hunters** that feed on other birds, fish, and small mammals.

- **Most birds of prey** are strong fliers, with sharp eyes, powerful talons (claws), and a hooked beak.

- **Birds of prey lay** a few eggs at a time. This makes them vulnerable to human egg collectors—one reason why many are endangered species.

- **Eagles** are the biggest of the hunting birds, with wing spans of up to 8ft (2.5m). The harpy eagle of the Amazon catches monkeys and sloths.

- **The American bald eagle** is not really bald, but has white feathers on its head.

- **There are two kinds of hawks**. Accipiters, like the goshawk, catch their prey by lying in wait on perches. Buteos, like the kestrel, hover in the air.

- **Buzzards** are buteo hawks.

- **In the Middle Ages**, merlins and falcons were trained to fly from a falconer's wrist to catch birds and animals.

> ★ STAR FACT ★
> The peregrine falcon can reach speeds of 220mph (350km/h) when diving on prey.

Frogs and toads

- **Frogs** and toads are amphibians: creatures that live both on land and in the water.

- **There are about 3,500 species** of frog and toad. Most live near water, but some live in trees and others live underground.

- **Frogs** are mostly smaller and better jumpers. Toads are bigger, with thicker, wartier skin which holds on to moisture and allows them to live on land longer.

- **Frogs and toads** are meat-eaters. They catch fast-moving insects by darting out their long, sticky tongues.

- **Frogs and toads begin life** as fish-like tadpoles, hatching in the water from huge clutches of eggs called spawn.

- **After 7 to 10 weeks**, tadpoles grow legs and lungs and develop into frogs ready to leave the water.

- **In midwife toads**, the male takes care of the eggs,

◀ *Frogs are superb jumpers, with long back legs to propel them into the air. Most also have suckers on their fingers to help them land securely on slippery surfaces.*

not the female, winding strings of eggs around his back legs and carrying them until they hatch.

- **The male Darwin's frog** swallows the eggs and keeps them in his throat until they hatch – and pop out of his mouth.

- **The goliath frog** of West Africa is the largest frog—at over 10in (25cm) long. The biggest toad is the cane toad of Queensland, Australia—one weighed 6lb (2.6kg) and measured more than 20in (50cm) in length.

- **The arrow-poison frogs** that live in the tropical rainforests of Central America get their name because natives tip their arrows with deadly poison from glands in the frogs' skin. Many arrow-poison frogs are very colorful, including some that are bright red.

Bats

- **Bats** are the only flying mammals. Their wings are made of leathery skin.

- **Most bats sleep** during the day, hanging upside down in caves, attics, and other dark places. They come out at night to hunt.

- **Bats find things** in the dark by giving out a series of high-pitched clicks. The bats tell where they are and locate (find) prey from the echoes (sounds that bounce back to them). This is called echolocation.

- **Bats are not blind,** their eyesight is as good as that of most humans.

- **There are 900 species** of bat, living on all continents except Antarctica.

- **Most bats feed** on insects, but fruit bats feed on fruit.

- **Many tropical flowers** rely on fruit bats to spread their pollen.

- **Frog-eating bats** can tell edible frogs from poisonous ones by the frogs' mating calls.

▶ *Bats spend their lives in darkness, finding their way with sounds so high-pitched only a young child can hear them.*

- **The vampire bats** of tropical Latin America feed on blood, sucking it from animals such as cattle and horses. A colony of 100 vampire bats can feed from the blood of 25 cows or 14,000 chickens in one night.

- **False vampire bats** are bats that do not suck on blood, but feed on other small creatures such as bats and rats. The greater false vampire bat of Southeast Asia is one of the biggest of all bats.

Animal senses

- **Animals** sense the world in a variety of ways, including by sight, hearing, touch, smell, and taste. Many animals have senses that humans do not have.

- **Sea creatures** rely on smell and taste, detecting tiny particles drifting in the water. For balance they often rely on simple balance organs called statocysts.

- **Sharks** have a better sense of smell than any other kind of fish. They can detect one part of animal blood in 100 million parts of water.

◀ *The slow loris is nocturnal, and its enormous eyes help it jump safely through forests in the darkness.*

- **For land animals,** sight is usually the most important sense. Hunting animals often have very sharp eyesight. Eagles, for instance, can see a rabbit moving from as far as 3mi (5km) away.

- **Owls** can hear sounds 10 times softer than a human can.

- **Male gypsy moths** can smell a mate over 7mi (11km) away.

- **Pit vipers** have special sensory pits (holes) on their heads which can pinpoint heat. This lets them track warm-blooded prey such as mice in pitch darkness.

- **The forked tongues** of snakes and lizards are used to taste the air and detect prey.

- **Cats' eyes** absorb 50 percent more light than human eyes, so they can see very well in the dark.

★ STAR FACT ★
Many butterflies can smell with special sense organs in their feet.

Lions

- **Lions** (along with tigers) are the biggest members of the cat family. Male lions may be 10ft (3m) long.

- **Lions used to live** through much of Europe and Asia. Now they are restricted to East and Southern Africa. Around 200 lions also live in the Gir forest in India.

- **Lions usually live** in grassland or scrub, in families called prides.

- **Lions are hunters** and they prey on antelopes, zebras, and even young giraffes. The lionesses (females) do most of the hunting.

- **Male lions** are easily recognizable because of their huge manes. There is usually more than one adult male in each pride and they usually eat before the lionesses and cubs.

★ **STAR FACT** ★
A lion can drag along a 66olb (300kg) zebra—it would take at least six men to do this.

The mane can be blonde, but gets darker with age

▲ To other lions, a male lion's shaggy mane makes him look even bigger and stronger, and protects him when fighting. A male lion is born without a mane. It starts growing when he is about two or three and is fully grown by the time he is five.

◀ Lion cubs live on milk at first, and eat their first meat after 50 days.

Cubs have very big paws for their size

▲ Female lions are called lionesses. They are slightly smaller than males but usually do most of the hunting, often in pairs. There are typically five to ten lionesses in each pride, and each one mates with the male when she is about three years old.

- **Lions usually catch** something to eat every four days or so. They can eat up to 90lb (40kg) in a single meal. Afterward they rest for 24 hours.

- **The lions in a pride** usually spend about 20 hours a day sleeping and resting, and they walk no farther than 6mi (10km) or so a day.

- **Lionesses catch their prey** not by speed, but by stealth and strength. They stalk their prey quietly, creeping close to the ground. Then, when it is about 50ft (15m) away, the lionesses make a sudden dash and pull the victim down with their strong forepaws.

- **Lionesses usually hunt** at dusk or dawn, but they have very good night vision, and so will often hunt in the dark.

- **Male lion cubs** are driven out of the pride when they are two years old. When a young male is fully grown, he has to fight an older male to join another pride.

Wading birds

- **Herons** are large wading birds that hunt for fish in shallow lakes and rivers. There are about 60 species.

- **When hunting**, a heron stands alone in the water, often on one leg, apparently asleep. Then it makes a lightning dart with its long beak to spear a fish or frog.

- **Herons** usually nest in colonies called heronries. They build loose stick-nests in trees.

- **Storks** are very large black-and-white water birds with long necks and legs. There are 17 species of stork.

- **The white stork** lives in Eurasia in the summer, and then migrates to Africa, India, and southern China in the winter.

- **White storks** build twig-nests on roofs, and some people think they bring luck to the house they nest on.

- **Flamingoes** are large pink wading birds which live in huge colonies on tropical lakes.

- **Spoonbills and ibises** are wading birds whose bills are sensitive enough to let them feel their prey moving in the water.

- **There are 28 species** of spoonbill and ibis.

- **The spoonbill's name** comes from its spoon-shaped bill, which it swings through the water to scoop up fish.

◀ Egrets are large wading birds that live in marshy areas, feeding on fish and insects.

Beetles

- **At least 250,000** species of beetle have been identified. They live everywhere on Earth, apart from in the oceans.

- **Unlike other insects**, adult beetles have a pair of thick, hard, front wings called elytra. These form an armor-like casing over the beetle's body.

- **The goliath beetle** of Africa is the heaviest flying insect, weighing over 3.5oz (100g) and growing to as much as 5in (13cm) long.

- **Dung beetles** roll away the dung of grazing animals to lay their eggs on. Fresh dung from one elephant may contain 7,000 beetles—they will clear the dung away in little more than a day.

- **A click beetle** can jump 12in (30cm) into the air.

> ★ **STAR FACT** ★
> The Arctic beetle can survive in temperatures
> below –76°F (–60°C).

- **The bombardier beetle** shoots attackers with jets of burning chemicals from the tip of its abdomen.

- **The rove beetle** can zoom across water on a liquid given off by glands on its abdomen.

- **The leaf-eating beetle** can clamp on to leaves using the suction of a layer of oil.

- **Stag beetles** have huge jaws which look like a stag's antlers.

Elytra (hard front wings)

▶ The jewel beetles of tropical South America get their name from the brilliant rainbow colors of their elytra (front wings).

Surviving the winter

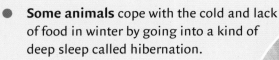

- **Some animals** cope with the cold and lack of food in winter by going into a kind of deep sleep called hibernation.

- **During hibernation**, an animal's body temperature drops and its heart rate and breathing slow, so it needs little energy to survive.

- **Small mammals** such as bats, squirrels, hamsters, hedgehogs, and chipmunks hibernate. So do birds such as nighthawks and swifts.

- **Reptiles** such as lizards and snakes go into torpor whenever the temperature gets too low. This state is similar to hibernation.

> ◀ Many mammals survive cold winters by hibernating. Some, like this Arctic fox, will sleep for a few days at a time when there is little food to be found.

- **Butterflies and other insects** go into a kind of suspended animation called diapause in winter.

- **The pika** (a small lagomorph) makes haystacks from grass in summer to provide food for the winter.

- **Beavers** collect branches in the fall and store them next to their lodges so they can feed on the bark during the winter.

- **Bears** go to sleep during winter, but not all scientists agree that they go into true hibernation.

- **Squirrels** bury dozens of stores of nuts in the fall to feed on during the winter. They seem to have a remarkable memory, as they are able to find each store when they need it.

> ★ STAR FACT ★
> Macaque monkeys in Japan keep warm in winter by bathing in hot volcanic springs.

Beavers

▶ In North America, beavers were once hunted so much that they were almost wiped out. They are now protected by law in some places.

- **Beavers are large rodents** (see Rabbits and rats) with flat, paddle-like tails. They live in northern America and northern Eurasia.

- **Beavers live** in rivers, streams, and lakes near woodlands and they are good swimmers, using their webbed feet as flippers and their tail as a rudder.

- **A beaver can swim underwater** for half a mile (almost 1km), holding its breath all the way.

- **Beavers can chop down** quite large trees with their

incredibly strong front teeth, gnawing around the tree in a ring until it finally crashes down.

- **Beavers feed on** bark as well as tree roots and shrubs. They are especially fond of poplars and willows.

- **Beavers build dams** across streams from tree branches laid on to a base of mud and stones. Families of beavers often work together on a dam.

- **Beaver dams** are 15–100ft (5–30m) long on average, but they can be up to 985ft (300m) long.

- **Beavers repair** their dams year after year, and some beaver dams are thought to be centuries old.

- **In the lake** behind the dam, beavers build a shelter called a lodge to live in during winter. Most lodges are like mini-islands made of branches and mud, with only a few underwater tunnels as entrances.

- **Beaver lodges** keep a beaver family so warm that in cold weather steam can often be seen rising from the ventilation hole.

Jellyfish

- **Jellyfish** are sea creatures with bell-shaped, jello-like bodies, and long stinging tentacles.

- **Biologists** call jellyfish medusa, after the mythical Greek goddess Medusa, who had wriggling snakes for hair.

- **Jellyfish** belong to the group called cnidarians.

- **Unlike anemones**, jellyfish float around freely, moving by squeezing water out from beneath their body. When a jellyfish stops squeezing, it slowly sinks.

- **A jellyfish's tentacles** are covered with stinging cells called nematocysts, which are used to catch fish and for protection. The stinging cells explode when touched, driving tiny poisonous threads into the victim.

- **Jellyfish vary in size** from a few millimetres to over 6ft (2m).

> ★ STAR FACT ★
> The box jellyfish has one of the deadliest poisons. It can kill a human in 30 seconds.

- **The bell of one giant jellyfish** measured 7.5ft (3m) across. Its tentacles were over 120ft (37m) long.

- **The Portuguese man-of-war** is not a true jellyfish, but a collection of hundreds of tiny animals called polyps which live together under a gas-filled float.

- **The purple jellyfish** can be red, yellow, or purple.

▼ *Jellyfish are among the world's most ancient animals.*

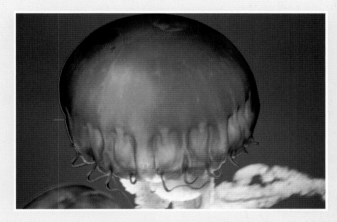

Otters

- **Otters** are small hunting mammals that are related to weasels. They are one of the 65 species of mustelid, along with stoats, skunks, and badgers.

- **Otters live** close to water and are excellent swimmers and divers.

- **Otters can close off** their nostrils and ears, allowing them to remain underwater for four or five minutes.

- **Otters are very playful creatures**, romping around on river banks and sliding down into the water.

- **Otters can use their paws** like hands, to play with things such as stones and shellfish.

- **Otters hunt fish**, mostly at night, but they also eat crayfish and crabs, clams, and frogs.

- **Otters usually live** in burrows in riverbanks.

- **Sea otters** live on the shores of western North America.

- **Sea otters will float** on their backs for hours, eating or sleeping. Mother sea otters often carry their baby on their stomachs while floating like this.

- **Sea otters eat shellfish**. They will balance a rock on their stomach while floating on their back, and crack the shellfish by banging it on the rock.

◀ *Sea otters float on their backs for hours in the seas off California and Alaska.*

Farm animals

- **Cattle** are descended from a creature called the wild auroch, which was tamed 9,000 years ago. There are now over 200 breeds of domestic cow.

- **Female cows** reared for milk, butter, and cheese production are called dairy cows. They give birth to a calf each year, and after it is born they provide milk twice a day.

- **A typical dairy cow** gives 4gal (16l) of milk a day, or 1,600gal (6,000l) a year.

- **Male cattle** are reared mainly for their meat, called beef. Beef breeds are usually heftier than dairy ones.

- **Sheep were first domesticated** over 10,000 years ago. There are now more than 700 million sheep in the world, and 800 different breeds.

◀ Female cattle are called cows, and males are called bulls. The young are calves. Female calves are also called heifers.

- **Hairy sheep** are kept for their milk and meat (lamb and mutton). Wooly sheep are kept for their wool.

- **Hens** lay one or two eggs a day— about 350 a year.

- **To keep hens laying**, their eggs must be taken from them every day. Otherwise the hens will try to nest so they can hatch them.

- **Turkeys** may have got their name from the mistaken idea that they came from Turkey.

> ★ STAR FACT ★
> When a cow chews the cud, the cud is food regurgitated from one of its four stomachs.

Colors and markings

▲ A zebra's stripes may seem to make it easy to see, but when it is moving they actually blur its outline and confuse predators.

- **Protective coloring** helps an animal hide from its enemies or warns them away.

- **Camouflage** is when an animal is colored to blend in with its surroundings, making it hard to see.

- **Ground nesting birds** like the nightjar are mottled brown, making them hard to spot among fallen leaves.

- **Wild pig and tapir babies** have striped and spotted fur making them hard to see in dappled jungle light.

- **Squid** can change their color to blend in with new surroundings.

- **Disruptive coloring** distorts an animal's body so that its real shape is disguised.

- **Bright colors** often warn predators that an animal is poisonous or tastes bad. For example, ladybugs are bright red and the cinnabar moth's caterpillars are black and yellow because they taste nasty.

- **Some creatures** mimic the colors of poisonous ones to warn predators off. Harmless hoverflies, for instance, look just like wasps.

- **Some animals** frighten off predators with coloring that makes them look much bigger. Peacock butterflies have big eyespots on their wings.

- **Courting animals**, especially male birds like the peacock, are often brightly colored to attract mates.

Crocodiles and alligators

- **Crocodiles, alligators, caimans, and gharials** are large reptiles that together form the group known as crocodilians. There are 14 species of crocodile, 7 alligators and caimans, and 1 gharial.

- **Crocodilian species** lived alongside the dinosaurs 200 million years ago, and they are the nearest we have to living dinosaurs today.

- **Crocodilians are hunters** that lie in wait for animals coming to drink at the water's edge. When crocodilians seize a victim they drag it into the water, stun it with a blow from their tail, then drown it.

- **Like all reptiles**, crocodilians get their energy from the sun. Typically, they bask in the sun on a sandbar or the river bank in the morning, then slip into the river at midday to cool off.

- **Crocodiles live** in tropical rivers and swamps. At over 16ft (5m) long, saltwater crocodiles are the world's largest reptiles—one grew to over 26ft (8m) long.

- **Crocodiles** are often said to cry after eating their victims. In fact only saltwater crocodiles cry, and they do it to get rid of salt, not because they are sorry.

- **Crocodiles have thinner snouts** than alligators, and a fourth tooth on the lower jaw which is visible when the crocodile's mouth is shut.

- **The female Nile crocodile** lays her eggs in nests which she digs in sandy river banks, afterward covering the eggs in sand to keep them at a steady temperature. When the babies hatch they make loud piping calls. The mother then digs them out and carries them one by one in her mouth to the river.

- **Alligators** are found both in the Florida Everglades in the United States and in the Yangtze River in China.

▼ Crocodiles often lurk in rivers, with just their eyes and nostrils visible above the water.

> ★ STAR FACT ★
> Crocodilians often swallow stones to help them stay underwater for long periods. Without this ballast, they might tip over.

A crocodile will often kill its victims with a swipe from its strong tail

The skin on its back has ridges formed by dozens of tiny bones called osteoderms

▶ Crocodiles are huge reptiles with powerful bodies, scaly skin, and great snapping jaws.

The crocodile's eyes and nostrils are raised so it can see and breathe while floating under water

The skin on its belly is smooth and was once prized as a material for shoes and handbags

Bears

- **Although bears** are the largest meat-eating land animals, they also eat many other foods, including fruits, nuts, and leaves.

- **The biggest bear** is the Alaskan brown bear, which grows to 9ft (2.7m) long and weighs up to 1,700lb (770lb).

- **There are seven species of bear**. Most live north of the equator, in all kinds of environments. Two live south of the equator—the spectacled bear in South America and the sun bear in Southeast Asia.

◄ *The polar bear has a white coat to camouflage it against the Arctic snow when it is hunting seals. Sometimes, only its black nose gives it away.*

★ STAR FACT ★
Bears are among the few animals to walk on the soles of their feet.

- **Bears do not hug** their prey to death, as is sometimes thought. Instead, they kill their victims with a powerful cuff from their front paws, or with their teeth.

- **The grizzly bear** is actually a brown bear with white fur on its shoulders. Grizzly bears from Alaska are the biggest brown bears, along with kodiak bears.

- **Polar bears mainly eat** seals and they are the only truly carnivorous bears.

- **Polar bears catch seals** when the seals poke their heads up through breathing holes in the Arctic ice.

- **Polar bears often swim underwater** and come up under an ice floe to tip seals off. They may also chuck huge chunks of ice at seals to stun them.

- **The sun bear** of Southeast Asia is the smallest bear.

Bees and wasps

▲ *Honey bees and bumble bees feed on pollen. They make honey from flower nectar to feed their young.*

- **Bees and wasps** are narrow-waisted insects (usually with hairy bodies). Many suck nectar from flowers.

- **There are 22,000 species of bee**. Some, like leaf-cutter bees, live alone. But most, like honey bees and bumble bees, live in vast colonies.

- **Honey bees** live in hives, either in hollow trees or in man-made beehive boxes. The inside of the hive is a honeycomb made up of hundreds of six-sided cells.

- **A honey bee colony** has a queen (the female bee that lays the eggs), tens of thousands of female worker bees, and a few hundred male drones.

- **Worker bees** collect nectar and pollen from flowers.

- **Each worker bee** makes ten trips a day and visits 1,000 flowers each trip. It takes 65,000 trips to 65 million flowers to make 2lb (1kg) of honey.

- **Honey bees** tell others where to find flowers rich in pollen or nectar by flying in a special dance-like pattern.

- **Wasps** do not make honey, but feed on nectar and fruit juice. Many species have a nasty sting in their tail.

- **Paper wasps build** huge papier maché nests the size of footballs, containing 15,000 or more cells.

- **Paper wasps make** papier-maché for their nest by chewing wood and mixing it with their spit.

Communication

    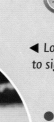

- **Crows** use at least 300 different croaks to communicate with each other. But crows from one area cannot understand crows from another one.

- **When two howler monkey troops** meet, the males scream at each other until one troop gives way.

- **The male orangutan** burps to warn other males to keep away.

- **Dogs** communicate through barks, yelps, whines, growls, and howls.

- **Many insects communicate** through the smell of chemicals called pheromones, which are released from special glands.

> ★ STAR FACT ★
> Using sign language, Coco the gorilla took an IQ test and got a score of 95.

◄ Lone wolves often howl at dusk or in the night to signal their ownership of a particular territory and to warn off rival wolves.

- **Tropical tree ant species** use ten different pheromones, combining them with different movements to send 50 different kinds of message.

- **A gorilla** named Coco was trained so that she could use over 1,000 different signs to communicate, each sign meaning different words. She called her pet cat "Soft good cat cat," and herself "Fine animal gorilla."

- **Female glow worms** communicate with males by making a series of flashes.

- **Many birds** are mimics and can imitate a whole variety of different sounds, including the human voice and machines like telephones (see Parrots and parakeets).

Parrots and parakeets

▲ The blue-and-yellow macaw of the Amazon rain forest has been trapped so much for the pet trade, it is now quite rare.

- **Parrots** are colorful birds with curved bills for eating fruits and seeds and for cracking nuts. They are very noisy birds and they live mostly in tropical rain forests.

- **Parrots** have feet with two toes pointing forward and two backward, allowing them to grip branches and hold food.

- **There are 330 or so parrot species** divided into three main groups —true parrots, cockatoos, and lories.

- **Half of all parrot species**, including macaws, green Amazon parrots, and parakeets, live in Latin America.

- **Australia and New Guinea** are home to parrots called cockatoos (which are white with feathered crests on their heads), as well as to lories and lorikeets.

- **The budgerigar** is a small parakeet from central Australia which is very popular as a pet.

- **The hanging parrots** of Southeast Asia get their name because they sleep upside down like bats.

- **The kea** of New Zealand is a parrot that eats meat as well as fruit. It was once wrongly thought to be a sheep killer.

- **Parrots** are well known for their mimicry of human voices. Some have a repertoire of 300 words or more.

- **An African gray parrot** called Alex was trained by scientist Irene Pepperberg to identify at least 50 different objects. Alex could ask for each of these objects in English—and also refuse them.

Ostriches and emus

▶ Ostriches live on the grasslands of Africa and nest in holes scooped out of the ground. The male scoops out the hole and leads several females to it to lay their eggs.

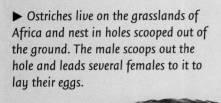

Bony crest

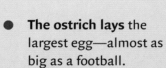

◀ The cassowary lives in the forests of tropical Australia and New Guinea. It has a crest which it uses like a crash helmet as it charges through the undergrowth.

Two toes with very sharp toenails

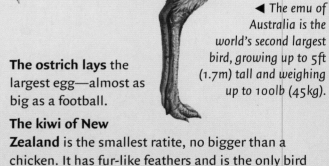

◀ The emu of Australia is the world's second largest bird, growing up to 5ft (1.7m) tall and weighing up to 100lb (45kg).

- **Ratites are big, flightless birds** like the ostrich, emu, cassowary, rhea, and kiwi. Ratites always walk or run everywhere, only using their small wings for balance and for show.

- **The ostrich** is the biggest living bird, towering up to 8ft (2.75m) in height and weighing over 330lb (150kg).

- **To escape a lion**, the ostrich can hurtle over the African savannah grasslands, where it lives, at speeds of 35mph (60km/h): faster than a racehorse. Even when the ostrich tires, its strong legs can still deliver a massive kick.

- **Ostriches** have only two toes on each foot, unlike the rhea of South America which has three.

- **The ostrich lays** the largest egg—almost as big as a football.

- **The kiwi of New Zealand** is the smallest ratite, no bigger than a chicken. It has fur-like feathers and is the only bird with nostrils at the tip of its bill, which it uses to sniff out worms and grubs.

- **The rare kakapo parrot** of New Zealand could fly once, but it lost the power of flight because it had no natural predators, until Europeans introduced dogs and cats to New Zealand.

- **The dodo** was a flightless bird that once lived on islands such as Mauritius in the Indian Ocean. It was wiped out in the 17th century when its eggs were eaten by pigs and monkeys imported by Europeans.

- **The emu** of Australia is the best swimmer of any flightless bird. Ostriches can swim well, too.

◀ Ostriches have soft downy plumage, but their head, neck and legs are almost bare.

Dogs and wolves

- **The dog family** is a large group of four-legged, long-nosed, meat-eating animals. It includes dogs, wolves, foxes, jackals, and coyotes.

- **All kinds of dog** have long canine teeth for piercing and tearing their prey. (Canine means "dog").

- **When hunting**, dogs rely mainly on their good sense of smell and acute hearing.

- **Wolves** are the largest wild dogs. They hunt together in packs to track down animals bigger than themselves, such as moose, deer, caribou, and musk oxen.

- **A wolf pack** may have 7 to 20 wolves, led by the eldest male and female.

- **A wolf pack's territory** may be 620 sq mi (1,000 sq km) or more. Wolves can travel vast distances when hunting.

- **Wolves once lived** all over Europe and North America, but are now rare in Europe and are found only in remote areas of North America as well as Asia.

- **Foxes** are cunning hunters which prowl at night, alone or in pairs. Typical prey includes rats, mice, and rabbits.

- **The red fox** has adapted to the growth of towns and cities and may often be seen at night raiding surburban garbage cans and dumps.

- **The jackals** of Africa look like small wolves, but they hunt alone for small prey and only meet in packs to grab the leftovers from the kill of a lion.

▶ Most wolves are gray wolves—either the timber wolf of cold forest regions, or the tundra wolf of the Arctic plains.

Poisonous insects

- **Insects are small**, but many have nasty poisons to protect themselves.

- **Most poisonous insects** are brightly colored—including many caterpillars, wasps and cardinal beetles—to warn off potential enemies .

- **Ants, bees, and wasps** have stings in their tails which they use to inject poison to defend themselves or paralyze prey.

- **Bee and wasp stings** have barbed ends to keep the sting in long enough to inject the poison. Honey bees cannot pull the barb out from human skins, and so tear themselves away and die.

- **Velvet ants** are not really ants at all, but wingless wasps with such a nasty sting that they are called "cow killers."

- **Ladybugs** make nasty chemicals in their knees.

- **When attacked**, swallowtail caterpillars whip out a smelly forked gland from a pocket behind their head and hit their attacker with it.

▲ Wasps poison their victims with the sharp sting in their tail.

- **The lubber grasshopper** is slow moving, but when attacked it oozes a foul smelling froth from its mouth and thorax.

- **The bombardier beetle** squirts out a spray of liquid from its rear end, almost like a small spray gun! This startles and stings the attacker and gives the small beetle time to esape.

Penguins

- **There are around 17 different species** of penguin, most of them living in huge colonies called rookeries along the coast of Antarctica and nearby islands.

- **Penguins** are superb swimmers, using their wings as flippers to push them through the water, and steering with their webbed feet.

- **Penguins' coats are** waterproofed with oil and thick fat so they can survive temperatures as low as −74°F (−60°C).

- **The smallest** is the fairy penguin, at 16in (40cm) high.

- **The emperor penguin** is the biggest swimming bird, at up to 4ft (1.2m) tall and weighing over 90lb (40kg) —twice the weight of any flying bird.

- **Emperor penguins** can dive briefly to depths of 275yd (250m) or more chasing fish, their main diet.

> ★ **STAR FACT** ★
> The male emperor penguin keeps the female's egg warm on his feet until it hatches.

▲ *Penguins are sociable birds that live in large colonies.*

- **Penguins** can leap high out of the water to land on an ice bank, but on land they can only waddle clumsily or toboggan along on their bellies.

- **Adélie penguins** waddle more than 200mi (320km) across the ice every year to reach their breeding ground.

- **When crossing the ice**, Adélie penguins steer by the sun. They lose their way when the sun goes down.

Iguanas

- **Iguanas** are large lizards that live around the Pacific and in the Americas.

- **Larger iguanas** are the only vegetarian lizards. Unlike other lizards, most eat fruit, flowers, and leaves, rather than insects.

- **The common iguana** lives high up in trees, but lays its eggs in a hole in the ground.

- **Common iguanas** will jump 20ft (6m) or more out of the trees to the ground if they are disturbed.

- **The rhinoceros iguana** of the West Indies gets its name from the pointed scales on its snout.

- **The marine iguana** of the Galapagos Islands is the only lizard that spends much of its life in the ocean.

- **Marine iguanas** keep their eggs warm ready for hatching in the mouth of volcanoes, risking death to put them there.

- **When in the water**, a marine iguana may dive for 15 minutes or more, pushing itself along with its tail.

- **Although marine iguanas** cannot breathe underwater, their heart rate slows so that they use less oxygen.

- **The chuckwalla** inflates its body with air to wedge itself in a rock crack if it is in danger.

◄ *Before each dive into water, marine iguanas warm themselves in the sun to gain energy.*

Crabs and lobsters

- **Crabs and lobsters** are part of an enormous group of creatures called crustaceans.

- **Most crabs and lobsters** have their own shell, but hermit crabs live inside the discarded shells of other creatures.

- **Crabs and lobsters are decapods**, which means they have ten legs, although the first pair are often strong pincers which are used to hold and tear food.

- **For spotting prey**, crabs and lobsters have two pairs of antennae on their heads and a pair of eyes on stalks.

- **One of a lobster's claws** usually has blunt knobs for crushing victims. The other has sharp teeth for cutting.

- **Male fiddler crabs** have one giant pincer which they waggle to attract a mate.

- **Robber crabs** have claws on their legs which they use to climb up trees to escape from predators.

- **The giant Japanese spider crab** can grow to 10ft (3m) across between the tips of its outstretched pincers.

- **When American spiny lobsters** migrate, they cling to each others' tails in a long line, marching for hundreds of miles along the seabed.

- **Sponge crabs** hide under sponges which they cut to fit. The sponge then grows at the same rate as the crab.

▼ Lobsters are dark green or blue when alive and only turn red when cooked.

Life in the desert

▲ Deserts like this are among the world's toughest environments for animals to survive.

- **In the Sahara Desert**, a large antelope called the addax survives without waterholes because it gets all its water from its food.

- **Many small animals** cope with the desert heat by resting in burrows or sheltering under stones during the day. They come out to feed only at night.

- **Desert animals** include many insects, spiders, scorpions, lizards, and snakes.

- **The dwarf puff adder** hides from the sun by burying itself in the sand until only its eyes show.

- **The fennec fox** and the antelope jack rabbit both lose heat through their ears. This way they keep cool.

- **The kangaroo rats** of California's Death Valley save water by eating their own droppings.

- **The Mojave squirrel** survives through long droughts by sleeping five or six days a week.

- **Swarms of desert locusts** can cover an area as big as 3,000 sq mi (5,000 sq km).

- **Sand grouse** fly hundreds of miles every night to reach watering holes.

★ STAR FACT ★
The African fringe-toed lizard dances to keep cool, lifting each foot in turn off the hot sand.

Finding a mate

- **Humans** are among the few animals that mate at any time of year. Most animals come into heat (are ready to mate) only at certain times.

- **Spring** is a common mating time. The warmer weather and longer hours of daylight trigger the production of sperm in males and eggs in females.

- **Some mammals**, such as bats, bears, and deer, have only one mating time a year. Others, such as rabbits, have many.

- **Many large mammals** pair for a short time, but a few (including beavers and wolves) pair for life. Some males (including lions and seals) have lots of mates.

- **To attract a mate**, many animals put on courtship displays such as special colors, songs and dances.

◀ Prairie dogs live in families called coteries, each made up of a male and several females.

- **The male capercaillies** (turkey-like birds) of Scotland attract a mate with clicks and rattles then a pop and a hiss.

- **Great crested grebes** perform dramatic dances in the water and present water plants to one another.

- **Male bower birds** paint their nests blue with berry juice and line them with blue shells and flowers to attract a mate.

- **Male birds of paradise** flash their bright feathers while strutting and dancing to attract a mate.

- **The male tern** catches a fish as a gift for the female. The male dancefly brings a dead insect which the female eats while mating.

Life in tropical grasslands

- **Tropical grasslands** are home to vast herds of grazing animals such as antelope and buffalo—and to the lions, cheetahs, and other big cats that prey on them.

- **There are few places to hide** on the grasslands, so most grassland animals are fast runners with long legs.

▼ With their long necks, giraffes can feed on the high branches of the thorn trees that dot the savanna grasslands of Africa.

★ STAR FACT ★
Cheetahs are the fastest runners in the world, reaching 70mph (110km/h) in short bursts.

- **Pronghorn** can run at 40mph (67km/h) for 10mi (16km).

- **There are more than 60 species** of antelope on the grasslands of Africa and southern Asia.

- **A century ago in South Africa**, herds of small antelopes called springboks could be as large as ten million strong and hundreds of miles long.

- **The springbok** gets its name from its habit of springing 10ft (3m) straight up in the air.

- **Grazing animals** are divided into perrisodactyls and artiodactyls, according to how many toes they have.

- **Perrisodactyls** have an odd number of toes on each foot. They include horses, rhinos, and tapirs.

- **Artiodactyls** have an even number. They include camels, buffaloes, deer, antelope, and cattle.

Elephants

- **There are three kinds** of elephant—the African forest elephant (Central and West Africa), the African savanna elephant (East and South Africa), and the Asian elephant (India and Southeast Asia).

- **African elephants** are the largest land animals, growing as tall as 13ft (4m) and weighing more than 13,000lb (6,000kg).

- **Asian elephants** are not as large as African elephants, and have smaller ears and tusks. They also have one "finger" on the tip of their trunk, while African elephants have two.

- **The scientific word** for an elephant's trunk is a proboscis. It is used like a hand to put food into the elephant's mouth, or to suck up water to squirt into its mouth or over its body to keep cool.

- **Elephants** are very intelligent animals, with the biggest brain of all land animals. They also have very good memories.

- **Female elephants**, called cows, live with their calves and younger bulls (males) in herds of 20 to 30 animals. Older bulls usually live alone.

- **Once a year**, bull elephants go into a state called musth (said "must"), when male hormones make them very wild and dangerous.

- **Elephants** usually live for about 70 years.

- **When an elephant dies**, its companions seem to mourn and cry.

▼ In dry areas, herds may travel vast distances to find food, with the bigger elephants protecting the little ones between their legs.

★ STAR FACT ★
Elephants use their trunks like snorkels when crossing deep rivers.

▼ When the leader of the herd senses danger, she lifts her trunk and sniffs the air—then warns the others by using her trunk to give a loud blast called a trumpet. If an intruder comes too close, she will roll down her trunk, throw back her ears, lower her head, and charge at up to 30mph (50 km/h).

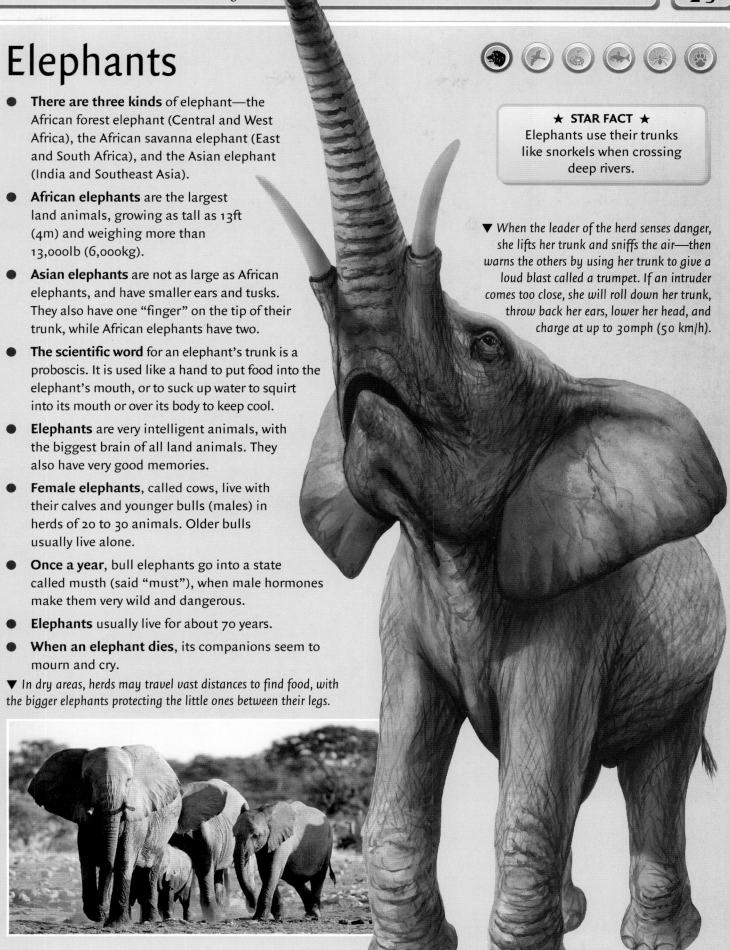

Camels

- **Camels** are the biggest desert mammals and they have adapted in many ways to help them live in extremely dry conditions.

- **Arabian camels** have one hump and live mainly in the Sahara Desert and the Middle East. Bactrian camels live in central Asia and have two humps.

- **A camel's hump** is made of fat, but the camel's body can break the fat down into food and water when these are scarce.

- **Camels can go** many days or even months without water. But when water is available, they can drink over 50gal (200l) in a day.

- **Camels sweat** very little, to save moisture.

▶ *The Arabian camel has been the "ship of the desert," transporting people and baggage, for thousands of years.*

Instead, their body temperature rises by as much as 43°F (6°C) when it is hot.

- **The camel's feet** have two joined toes to stop them from sinking into soft sand (Arabian camels) or soft snow (Bactrians).

- **The camel's nostrils** can close up completely to block out sand.

- **Camels have** a double row of eyelashes to protect their eyes from sand and sun.

- **The camel's stomach** is huge, with three different sections. Like cows, camels are ruminants —this means they partially digest food, then bring it back into their mouths to chew the cud.

★ **STAR FACT** ★
Camels have by far the worst smelling breath in the entire animal kingdom.

Eating food

▲ *Bears are omnivores, eating fish and other meat, although they will eat berries, leaves, and almost anything when hungry.*

- **Herbivores** are animals that usually eat only plants.

- **Carnivores** are animals that eat animal flesh (meat).

- **Omnivores** eat plants and animals. Many primates such as monkeys, apes, and humans are omnivorous.

- **Insectivores** eat insects. Some, such as bats and shrews, have teeth for breaking through insects' shells. Others, such as anteaters, have long, sticky tongues for licking up ants and termites, but few or no teeth.

- **Herbivores** such as cattle, elephants, and horses either graze (eat grass) or browse (eat mainly leaves, bark, and the buds of bushes and trees).

- **Herbivores** have tough, crowned teeth to cope with their plant food.

- **Carnivores** have pointed canine teeth for tearing meat.

- **Some carnivores**, such as hyenas, do not hunt and instead feed on carrion (the remains of dead animals).

- **Herbivores** eat for much of the time. However, because meat is very nourishing, carnivores eat only occasionally and tend to rest after each meal.

- **Every living thing** is part of a food chain, in which it feeds on the living thing before it in the chain and is in turn eaten by the living thing next to it in the chain.

Dolphins

- **Dolphins** are sea creatures that belong to the same family as whales: the cetaceans.

- **Dolphins are mammals**, not fish. They are warm-blooded, and mothers feed their young on milk.

- **There are two kinds** of dolphin—marine (sea) dolphins (32 species) and river dolphins (5 species).

- **Dolphins usually live** in groups of 20 to 100 animals.

- **Dolphins take care of** each other. Often, they will support an injured companion on the surface.

- **Dolphins communicate** with high-pitched clicks called phonations. Some clicks are higher than any other animal noise and humans cannot hear them.

- **Dolphins use sound** to find things and can identify different objects even when blindfolded.

> ★ STAR FACT ★
> Dolphins have rescued drowning humans by pushing them to the surface.

▲ *Dolphins are among the most intelligent of the animals, along with humans and chimpanzees.*

- **Dolphins can be trained** to jump through hoops, toss balls, or "walk" backward through the water on their tails.

- **Bottle-nosed dolphins** get their name from their short beaks (which also make them look like they are smiling). They are friendly and often swim near boats.

Pheasants and peafowl

- **A game bird** is a bird that is hunted for sport.

- **Game birds** spend most of the time strutting along the ground looking for seeds. They fly only in emergencies.

- **There are 250 species** of game bird, including pheasants, grouse, partridges, quails, wild turkeys, and peafowl.

- **Most of the 48 species** of pheasant originated in China and central Asia.

- **Many hen (female) game birds** have dull brown plumage that helps them to hide in their woodland and moorland homes.

- **Many cock (male) game birds** have very colorful plumage to attract mates.

- **In the breeding season**, cocks strut and puff up their plumage to attract a mate. They also draw attention to themselves by cackling, whistling, and screaming.

- **Pheasant cocks** often fight each other violently to win a particular mating area.

- **The jungle fowl** of Southeast Asia is the wild ancestor of the domestic chicken.

- **Peacocks** were carried as treasures from India throughout the ancient world.

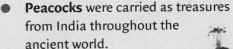

◀ *The peacock (the male peafowl) of India and Sri Lanka is the most spectacular of all pheasants. When courting the drab peahen, the peacock throws up his tail feathers to create a gigantic turquoise fan.*

Kangaroos and koalas

- **Kangaroos** are big Australian mammals that hop around on their hind (back) legs.

- **A kangaroo's tail** can be over 5ft (1.5m) long. It is used for balance when hopping, and to hold it up when walking.

- **Red kangaroos** can hop at 35mph (55km/h) for short distances.

- **Red kangaroos** can leap 30ft (9m) forward in one huge bound, and jump fences that are 6–10ft (2–3m) high.

- **There are two kinds of kangaroo**: red kangaroos and gray kangaroos. Red kangaroos live in the dry grasslands of central Australia. Gray kangaroos live in the southeast, in woods and grassland.

- **Kangaroos are marsupials,** animals whose babies are born before they are ready to survive in the outside word and so live for a while protected in a pouch on their mother's belly.

▲ Koalas drink very little water, and their name comes from an Aboriginal word for "no drink."

- **Koalas** are Australian mammals that look like teddy bears, but which are no relation to any kind of bear.

- **Like kangaroos**, koalas are marsupials. A koala baby spends 6 months in its mother's pouch and another 6 months riding on her back.

- **Koalas** spend 18 hours a day sleeping. The rest of the time they feed on the leaves of eucalyptus trees.

- **Other Australian marsupials** include the wombat, and several kinds of wallaby (which look like small kangaroos), and bandicoots (which looks like rats).

▼ When they are first born, kangaroos are naked and very tiny—just an inch or so long, with two tiny arms. But right away they have to haul themselves up through the fur on their mother's belly and into her pouch. Here the baby kangaroo (called a joey) lives and grows for 6 to 8 months, sucking on teats inside the pouch. Only when it is quite large and covered in fur will it pop out of the pouch to live by itself.

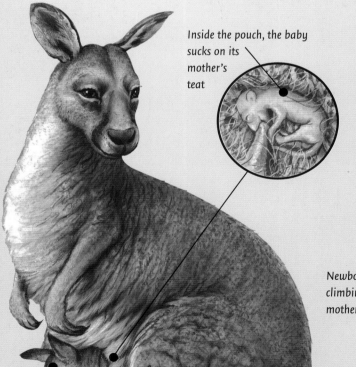

Inside the pouch, the baby sucks on its mother's teat

Young kangaroo or "joey"

Newborn kangaroo climbing up its mother's belly

Entrance to pouch

Newborn kangaroo

Mother kangaroo's birth canal

Migration

- **Migration** is when animals move from one place to another to avoid the cold or to find food and water.

- **Some migrations** are daily, some are seasonal, and some are permanent.

- **Starlings** migrate every day from the country to their roosts in the city.

- **Many birds, whales, seals, and bats** migrate closer to the tropics in the fall to escape the winter cold.

- **One knot** (a kind of small bird) took just eight days to fly 3,500mi (5,600km), from Britain to West Africa.

- **Barheaded geese** migrate over the top of the Himalayan mountains, flying as high as 26,000ft (8,000m).

- **Migrating birds** are often brilliant navigators. Bristle-thighed curlews find their way from Alaska to tiny islands in the Pacific 5,600mi (9,000km) away.

- **Shearwaters**, sparrows, and homing pigeons are able to fly home when released by scientists in strange places, thousands of miles away.

▶ In summer, moose spend most of the time alone. But in winter they gather and trample areas of snow (called yards) to help each other get at the grass beneath.

- **The Arctic tern** is the greatest migrator, flying 18,600mi (30,000km) from the Arctic to the Antarctic and back again each year.

- **Monarch butterflies** migrate 2,500mi (4,000km) every year, from North America to small clumps of trees in Mexico. Remarkably, the migrating butterflies have never made the journey before.

Eels

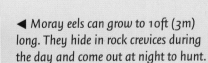

- **Eels** are long, slimy fish that look like snakes.

- **Baby eels** are called elvers.

- **Some eels** live in rivers, but most live in the sea, including moray eels and conger eels.

- **Moray eels** are huge and live in tropical waters, hunting fish, squid, and cuttlefish.

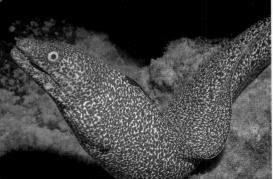

- **Gulper eels** can live more than 2.8mi (4.5km) down in the Atlantic Ocean. Their mouths are huge to help them catch food in the dark, deep water—so big that they can swallow fish larger than themselves whole.

- **Every fall**, some European common eels migrate more than 7,000km (4,500mi), from the Baltic Sea in Europe to the Sargasso Sea near the West Indies to lay their eggs.

◀ Moray eels can grow to 10ft (3m) long. They hide in rock crevices during the day and come out at night to hunt.

- **Migrating eels** are thought to find their way partly by detecting weak electric currents created by the movement of the water.

- **When European eels** hatch in the Sargasso Sea they are carried northeast by the ocean current, developing as they go into tiny transparent eels called glass eels.

- **Electric eels** of South America can produce an electric shock of over 500 volts: enough to knock over an adult human.

- **Garden eels** live in colonies on the seabed, poking out from holes in the sand to catch food drifting by. Their colonies look like gardens of weird plants.

What are mammals?

- **Mammals** are animals with furry bodies, warm blood, and a unique habit of suckling their young on milk from the mother's teats.

- **Humans and most other mammals** keep their body temperatures at around 98.6°F (36°C).

- **Fur and fat** protect mammals from the cold. When they do get cold, they curl up, seek shelter, or shiver.

- **All mammals** except monotremes (see Strange mammals) give birth to live young.

- **Most mammals** are placental, their young are nourished inside the mother's womb through an organ called the placenta until they are fully developed.

- **Marsupials** are not placental. Their young develop mainly in the mother's pouch (see Kangaroos and koalas).

- **The time from mating to birth** is called the gestation period. In mammals, it varies from 20 days for some mice to 22 months for elephants.

▲ *Pigs have 12 or so babies in a litter and seven pairs of teats.*

- **Marsupials** have short pregnancies—the opossum's is just 12 days.

- **Mammals** vary in size from the finger-sized Etruscan shrew to the 100ft (30m) long blue whale.

- **One of the earliest mammals** was Megazostrodon, a tiny shrew-like creature. It lived alongside the dinosaurs about 120 million years ago.

Ocean fish

◀ *Flying fish beat their tails so fast they are able to "fly" away from predators.*

- **Nearly 75 percent** of all fish live in the seas and oceans.

- **The biggest, fastest swimming fish**, such as swordfish and marlin, live near the surface of the open ocean, far from land. They often migrate vast distances to spawn (lay their eggs) or find food.

- **Many smaller fish** live deeper down, including seabed-dwellers like eels and flatfish (such as plaice, turbot, and flounders).

- **All flatfish** start life as normal-shaped fish, but as they grow older, one eye slowly slides around the head to join the other. The pattern of scales also changes so that one side is the top and one side is the bottom.

- **Plaice** lie on the seabed on their left side, while turbot lie on their right side. Some flounders lie on their left and some on their right.

- **The upper side** of a flatfish is usually camouflaged to help it blend in with the sea floor.

- **In the temperate waters** of the Atlantic there are rich fishing grounds for fish such as herring.

- **The swordfish** can swim at up to 50mph (80km/h). It uses its long spike to slash or stab squid.

- **The bluefin tuna** can grow to as long as 10ft (3m) and weigh more than 1,100lb (500kg). It is also a fast swimmer—one crossed the Atlantic in 199 days.

> ★ **STAR FACT** ★
> Flying fish can glide for 437yd (400m) and soar up to 20ft (6m) above the waves.

Grasshoppers and crickets

- **Grasshoppers** are plant-eating insects related to crickets, locusts, and katydids.

- **Grasshoppers** belong to two main families—short-horned, which includes locusts, and long-horned, which includes katydids and crickets.

- **Short-horned grasshoppers** have ears on the side of their body. Long-horned grasshoppers have ears in their knees.

- **Grasshoppers** have powerful back legs, which allow them to jump huge distances.

- **Some grasshoppers** can leap more than 10ft (3m).

- **Grasshoppers** sing by rubbing their hind legs across their closed forewings.

- **A grasshopper's singing** is called stridulation.

- **Crickets** chirrup faster the warmer it is.

- **If you count** the number of chirrups a snowy tree cricket gives in 15 seconds, then add 40, you get the temperature in degrees Fahrenheit.

> ★ STAR FACT ★
> A frightened lubber grasshopper oozes a horrible smelling froth from its mouth.

▼ *The spikes on the long-horned grasshopper's back legs are what make the chirruping sound as it rubs them against its forewings.*

Life in the mountains

- **Mountains** are cold, windy places where only certain animals can survive—including agile hunters such as pumas and snow leopards, and nimble grazers such as mountain goats, yaks, ibex, and chamois.

- **The world's highest-living** mammal is the yak, a type of wild cattle which can survive more than 20,000ft (6,000m) up in the Himalayas.

- **Mountain goats** have hooves with sharp edges that dig into cracks in the rock, and hollow soles that act like suction pads.

- **In winter**, the mountain goat's pelage (coat) turns white, making it hard to spot against the snow.

- **The Himalayan snowcock** nests higher than almost any other bird, often above 13,000ft (4,000m).

▲ *Sheep like these dall sheep are well equipped for life in the mountains, with their thick coats and nimble feet.*

- **The Alpine chough** has been seen flying at 27,000ft (8,200m) up on Everest.

- **Lammergeiers** are the vultures of the African and southern European mountains. They break tough bones, when feeding, by dropping them from a great height on to stones and then eating the marrow.

- **The Andean condor** of the South American Andes is a gigantic scavenger which can carry off deer and sheep. It is said to dive from the skies like a fighter plane (see also vultures).

- **The puma**, or mountain lion, can jump well over 16.5ft (5m) up on to a rock ledge, that is like you jumping into an upstairs window.

- **The snow leopard** of the Himalayan mountains is now one of the rarest of all the big cats, because it has been hunted almost to extinction for its beautiful fur coat.

Life in the oceans

▲ Many kinds of fish and other sea creatures live in the sunlit zone near the surface of the oceans.

- **Oceans** cover 70 percent of the Earth and they are the largest single animal habitat.

- **Scientists divide the ocean** into two main environments—the pelagic (which is the water itself), and the benthic (which is the seabed).

- **Most benthic animals** live in shallow waters around the continents. They include worms, clams, crabs, and lobsters, as well as bottom-feeding fish.

- **Scientists call the sunny surface waters** the euphotic zone. This extends down 500ft (150m) and is where billions of plankton (microscopic animals and plants) live.

- **Green plant plankton** (algae) of the oceans produce 30 percent of the world's vegetable matter each year.

- **Animal plankton** include shrimps and jellyfish.

- **The surface waters** are also home to squid, fish, and mammals such as whales.

- **Below the surface zone**, down to about 6,500ft (2,000m), is the twilight bathyal zone. There is too little light for plants to grow, but many hunting fish and squid live.

- **Below 6,500ft (2,000m)** is the dark abyssal zone, where only weird fish like gulper eels and anglerfish live (see Strange sea creatures).

- **The Sargasso** is a vast area in the West Atlantic where seaweed grows thick. It is a rich home for barnacles and other sea creatures.

Corals and anemones

- **Sea anemones** are tiny, meat-eating animals that look a bit like flowers. They cling to rocks and catch tiny prey with their tentacles (see Life on the shore).

- **Coral reefs** are the undersea equivalent of rain forests, teeming with fish and other ocean life. They are built by tiny, sea anemone-like animals called polyps.

- **Coral polyps** live all their lives in just one place, either attached to a rock or to dead polyps.

- **When coral polyps die**, their cup-shaped skeletons become hard coral.

- **Coral reefs** are long ridges, mounds, towers, and other shapes made from billions of coral polyps and their skeletons.

- **Fringing reefs** are shallow coral reefs that stretch out from the seashore.

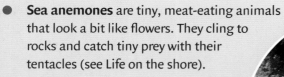

◄ Sea anemones look like flowers, with petals, but are actually carnivorous animals with rings of tentacles.

- **Barrier reefs** form a long, underwater wall a little way offshore.

- **The Great Barrier Reef** off eastern Australia is the longest reef in the world, stretching over 1,200mi (2,000 km).

- **Coral atolls** are ring-shaped islands that formed from fringing reefs around an old volcano (which has long since sunk beneath the waves).

- **Coral reefs** take millions of years to form—the Great Barrier Reef is 18 million years old, for example. By drilling a core into ancient corals, and analyzing the minerals and growth rate, scientists can read of the oceans history back for millions of years.

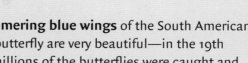

Butterflies

- **Butterflies** are insects with four large wings. They feed either on the nectar of flowers or on fruit.

- **Together with moths**, butterflies make up the scientific order Lepidoptera—the word means "scaly wings." There are more than 165,000 species of Lepidoptera: 20,000 butterflies and 145,000 moths.

- **Many butterflies** are brightly colored and fly by day. They have slim, hairless bodies and club-shaped antennae (feelers).

- **The biggest butterfly** is the Queen Alexandra's birdwing of New Guinea, with 10in (25cm) wide wings. The smallest is the Western pygmy blue.

- **Butterflies can only fly** if their wing muscles are warm. To warm up, they bask in the sun so their wings soak up energy like solar panels.

- **The monarch butterfly** is such a strong flier it can cross the Atlantic Ocean (see Migration).

- **The shimmering blue wings** of the South American morpho butterfly are very beautiful—in the 19th century millions of the butterflies were caught and made into brooches.

- **Most female butterflies** live only a few days, so they have to mate and lay eggs quickly. Most males court them with elaborate flying displays.

- **Butterflies** taste with their tarsi (feet). Females "stamp" on leaves to see if they are ripe enough for egg laying.

- **Every butterfly's caterpillar** has its own chosen food plants, different from the flowers the adult feeds on.

▲ Every species of butterfly has its own wing pattern, like a fingerprint — some drab like this, others brilliantly colored.

1. **Egg**—eggs are laid on plants that will provide food when the caterpillars hatch

2. **Larva**—when the caterpillar hatches, it begins eating and growing right away

3. **Pupa**—butterfly caterpillars develop hard cases and hang from a stem or leaf

4. **Metamorphosis**—it takes a few days to a year for the pupa to turn into an adult

◄ Few insects change as much as butterflies do during their lives. Butterflies start off as an egg, then hatch into a long, wiggly larva called a caterpillar, which eats leaves greedily and grows rapidly. When it is big enough, the caterpillar makes itself a case, which can be either a cocoon or a chrysalis. Inside, it metamorphoses (changes) into an adult, then breaks out, dries its new wings, and flies away.

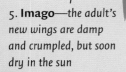

5. **Imago**—the adult's new wings are damp and crumpled, but soon dry in the sun

★ STAR FACT ★
Butterflies fly like no other insects, flapping their wings like birds.

Octopuses and squid

- **Octopuses and squid** belong to a family of mollusks called cephalopods.

- **Octopuses** are sea creatures with a round, soft, boneless body, three hearts, and eight long arms called tentacles.

- **An octopus's tentacles** are covered with suckers that allow it to grip rocks and prey.

- **Octopuses** have two large eyes, similar to humans, and a beak-like mouth.

- **When in danger** an octopus may send out a cloud of inky black fluid. Sometimes the ink cloud is the same shape as the octopus and may fool a predator into chasing the cloud.

> ★ STAR FACT ★
> The blue-ringed octopus's poison is so deadly
> that it kills more people than sharks.

- **Some octopuses can change color** dramatically to startle a predator or blend in with its background.

- **The smallest octopus** is just 1in (2.5cm) across. The biggest measures 20ft (6m) across.

- **A squid** has eight arms and two tentacles and swims by forcing a jet of water out of its body.

- **Giant squid** in the Pacific can be 60ft (18m) or more long.

◀ *Most of the hundreds of species of octopus live on the beds of shallow oceans around the world. Octopuses are quite intelligent creatures.*

Life on the grasslands

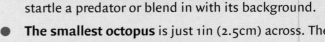

▲ *Until they were wiped out by European settlers, vast herds of bison (buffalo) roamed the North American prairies.*

- **Grasslands** form in temperate (moderate temperature) regions where there is too little rainfall for forests, but enough to allow grass to grow.

- **Temperate grasslands** include the prairies of North America, the pampas of South America, the veld of South Africa, and the vast steppes of Eurasia.

- **There is little cover** on grasslands, so many grassland animals have very good eyesight and large ears to detect predators from afar.

- **Some grassland animals escape** from predators by speed. These include jack rabbits, deer, pronghorn antelopes, wild asses, and flightless birds like the emu.

- **Some animals**, such as mice and prairie dogs, escape by hiding underground in burrows.

- **Some birds hide** by building their nests in bushes. These include meadowlarks, quails, and blackbirds.

- **The main predators** are dogs like the coyote and fox.

- **The North American prairies** have a small wild cat called the bobcat.

- **Prairie dogs** live in huge underground colonies called towns. One contained 400 million animals and covered over 37,000 sq mi (60,000 sq km).

- **When they meet**, prairie dogs kiss each other to find out whether they are from the same group.

Seagulls and albatrosses

▲ *Seagulls catch small fish, steal eggs and young from other birds, scavenge on waste, and sometimes fly inland to find worms.*

- **Gulls are big seabirds** that live on coasts all around the world, nesting on cliffs, islands, or beaches.

- **Gulls are related** to skuas and terns.

- **Skuas** have hooked claws and sharp bills, which they

★ STAR FACT ★
Herring gulls watch ducks diving for fish and then steal it when the ducks resurface.

use to attack other birds and force them to disgorge (throw up) their food, which the skua then eats.

- **Skuas are such good acrobats** that they can catch the disgorged meal of another bird in mid-air.

- **The great skua** often pounces on seagulls, drowns them, and then steals their chicks.

- **Wandering albatrosses** are the biggest of all seabirds, with white bodies and dark wings.

- **The wandering albatross** has the biggest wingspan of any bird—12ft (3.7m) across.

- **An albatross** will often follow a ship for days without stopping to rest.

- **Wild albatrosses** may live for more than 50 years.

Giraffes

- **Giraffes** are the tallest mammals, growing to more than 16.5ft (5m). Their height allows them to reach and eat the leaves and fruit at the tops of trees.

- **A giraffe's legs** are almost 6.5ft (2m) long. Their long legs mean when they run they can gallop faster than the speediest racehorse.

- **A giraffe's neck** may be over 6.5ft (2m) long, but it only has seven bones—the same number as humans.

- **Giraffes live** in Africa, south of the Sahara, in bush country.

- **The giraffe's long tongue** is so tough that it can wrap around the thorns of a thorn tree to grab twigs.

- **When drinking**, a giraffe has to spread its forelegs wide or kneel down to reach

▲ *Giraffes are the world's tallest animals, but they are five times as light as elephants.*

the water. This position makes it very vulnerable to attack by lions.

- **When giraffes walk**, they move the two legs on one side of their body, then the two on the other side.

- **A giraffe's coat** is patched in brown on cream, and each giraffe has its own unique pattern. The reticulated giraffes of East Africa have triangular patches, but the South African Cape giraffes have blotchy markings.

- **During breeding time**, rival males rub their necks together and swing them from side to side. This is called necking.

- **When first born**, a baby giraffe is very wobbly on its legs and so cannot stand up for at least its first half an hour.

Whales

- **Whales**, dolphins, and porpoises are large mammals called cetaceans that live mostly in the seas and oceans. Dolphins and porpoises are small whales.

- **Like all mammals**, whales have lungs: this means they have to come to the surface to breathe every 10 minutes or so, although they can stay down for up to 40 minutes. A sperm whale can hold its breath for 2 hours.

- **Whales breathe** through blowholes on top of their head. When a whale breathes out, it spouts out water vapor and mucus. When it breathes in, it sucks in about 500gal (2,000l) of air within about 2 seconds.

- **Like land mammals**, whales nurse their babies with their own milk. Whale milk is so rich that babies grow incredibly fast. Blue whale babies are over 25ft (7m) long when they are born and gain an extra 220lb (100kg) or so a day for about seven months.

▶ *Killer whales or orcas are big deep sea predators, growing to as long as 30ft (9m) and weighing up to 10 tons. They feed on fish, seals, penguins, and dolphins.*

Dorsal fin

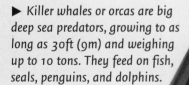

To swim, whales flap their fluke (tail) up and down

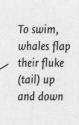

▲ *Humpback whales live together in groups called pods and keep in touch with their own "dialect" of noises.*

- **Toothed whales**, such as the sperm whale and the orca or killer whale, have teeth and prey on large fish and seals. The six groups of toothed whale are sperm whales, beaked whales, belugas and narwhals, dolphins, porpoises, and river dolphins.

- **Baleen whales**, such as the humpback and blue, have a comb of thin plates called baleen in place of teeth. They feed by straining small, shrimp-like creatures called krill through their baleen. There are five baleen whale groups, including right whales, gray whales, and rorquals. Rorquals have grooves on their throats and include humpback, minke, and blue whales.

> ★ **STAR FACT** ★
> Male humpbacks make elaborate "songs" lasting 20 minutes or more—perhaps to woo females.

- **The blue whale** is the largest creature that ever lived. Blue whales grow to be over 100ft (30m) long and weigh more than 150 tons. In summer, they eat over 4 tons of krill every day—that is 4 million krill.

- **Whales keep in touch** with sounds called phonations. Large baleen whales make sounds which are too low for humans to hear, but they can be heard by other whales at least 50mi (80km) away.

- **Most baleen whales** live alone or in small groups, but toothed whales, especially dolphins, often swim together in groups called pods or schools.

What are birds?

- **Not all birds** can fly, but they all have feathers.
- **Feathers** are light, but they are linked by hooks called barbs to make them strong enough for flight.
- **Wrens** have 1,000 feathers, while swans have 20,000.
- **Birds have four kinds** of wing feather: large primaries, smaller secondaries, coverts, and contours.
- **Every kind of bird** has its own formation pattern and color of feathers, called its plumage.
- **Instead of teeth**, birds have a hard beak or bill.
- **Unlike humans**, birds do not give birth to babies. Instead they lay eggs, usually sitting on them to keep them warm until they hatch (see birds' nests and eggs).
- **Birds fly in two ways**: by gliding with their wings

> ★ STAR FACT ★
> Birds may be descended from dinosaurs and took to the air about 150 million years ago.

▲ *Most birds flap their wings to fly. Even birds that spend much of their time gliding have to flap their wings to take off and land.*

held still, or by flapping their wings up and down.

- **Gliding is less effort** than flapping, and birds that stay in the air a long time tend to be superb gliders, including birds of prey, swifts, gulls, and gannets.
- **Albatrosses and petrels** have long narrow wings that help them sail upward on rising air currents.

Life in rivers and lakes

- **Rivers, lakes,** and other freshwater habitats are home to all sorts of fish, including bream and trout.
- **Fast-flowing streams** are preferred by fish such as trout and grayling. Slow-flowing rivers and lakes are home to tench, rudd, and carp.

▲ *Upland lakes like these are home to many fish, including char, powan, and bullhead. Fish such as brown trout swim in the streams that tumble down into the lake.*

- **Some fish feed** on floating plant matter, while others take insects from the surface of the water.
- **Common bream and berbel** hunt on the riverbed, eating insect larvae, worms, and mollusks.
- **Perch and pike** are predators of lakes and slow-flowing rivers.
- **Pike are the sharks** of the river, deadly hunters that lurk among weeds waiting for unwary fish, or even rats and birds. Pike can weigh as much as 65lb (30kg).
- **Mammals of rivers and lakes** include voles, water rats, and otters.
- **Birds of rivers and lakes** include birds that dive for fish (such as kingfishers), small wading birds (such as redshanks, avocets, and curlews), large wading birds (such as herons, storks, and flamingos), and waterfowl (such as ducks, swans, and geese).
- **Insects** include dragonflies and water boatmen.
- **Amphibians** include frogs and newts.

Cobras and vipers

◀ *When on the defensive, a cobra rears up and spreads the skin of its neck in a hood to make it look bigger. This often gives victims a chance to hit it away.*

- **Two kinds of poisonous snake** are dangerous to humans, vipers and elapids such as cobras and mambas.

- **Elapids** have their venom (poison) in short front fangs. A viper's fangs are so long that they usually have to be folded away.

- **The hamadryad cobra** of Southeast Asia, the world's largest poisonous snake, grows to over 16ft (5m).

> ★ STAR FACT ★
> Fer-de-lance snakes have 60 to 80 babies, each of which is deadly poisonous.

- **In India, cobras kill** more than 7,000 people every year. The bite of a king cobra can kill an elephant in 4 hours. The marine cobra lives in the ocean and its venom is 100 times more deadly.

- **Snake charmers** use the spectacled cobra, playing to it so that it follows the pipe as if about to strike, but the snake's fangs have been removed to make it safe.

- **A spitting cobra** squirts venom into its attacker's eyes, and is accurate at 6ft (2m) or more. The venom is not deadly, but it blinds the victim and is very painful.

- **The black mamba** of Africa can race along at 15mph (25km/h) with its head raised and its tongue flickering.

- **A viper's venom** kills its victims by making their blood clot. Viper venom has been used to treat hemophiliacs (people whose blood does not clot well).

- **The pit vipers** of the Americas hunt their warm-blooded victims using heat-sensitive pits on the side of their heads (see Animal senses).

Horses

- **Horses** are big, four-legged, hooved animals, now bred mainly for human use.

- **Male horses** are stallions, females are mares, babies are foals, and young males are colts.

- **The only wild horse** is the Przewalski of central Asia.

- **The mustangs** (wild horses) of the U.S.A. are descended from tame horses.

▲ *All horses, wild and tame, may be descended from the prehistoric Merychippus (see Evolution).*

- **Tame horses** are of three main kinds: light horses for riding (such as Morgans and Arabs), heavy horses for pulling plows and wagons (such as Pecherons and Suffolk punches), and ponies (such as Shetlands).

- **Most racehorses and hunting horses** are thoroughbred (pure) Arab horses descended from just three stallions that lived around 1700: Darley Arabian, Godolphin Barb, and Byerly Turk.

- **Lippizaners** are beautiful white horses, the best-known of which are trained to jump and dance at the Spanish Riding School in Vienna.

- **The shire horse** is probably the largest horse, bred after Henry VIII had all horses under 5ft (1.5m) destroyed.

- **You can tell a horse's age** by counting its teeth—a one-year-old has six pairs, a 5-year-old has 12.

- **Quarter horses** are agile horses used by cowhands for cutting out (sorting cows from the herd). They got their name from running quarter-mile races.

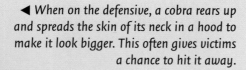

Seals and sea lions

- **Seals, sea lions, and walruses** are sea mammals that mainly live in water and are agile swimmers, but which waddle awkwardly when they come on land.

- **Most seals** eat fish, squid, and shellfish. Crabeater seals eat mainly shrimps, not crabs.

- **Seals and sea lions** have ears, but only sea lions (and fur seals) have ear flaps.

> ★ STAR FACT ★
> The 13ft (4m) long leopard seal of Antarctica feeds on penguins and even other seals.

- **Only sea lions** can move their back flippers under their body when travelling about on land.

- **When seals come ashore** to breed, they live for weeks in vast colonies called rookeries.

- **Walruses** are bigger and bulkier than seals, and they have massive tusks and face whiskers.

- **When hunters kill seal pups** for their fur, or to keep numbers down, it is called culling.

- **Elephant seals** spend up to 8 months far out in the ocean continuously diving, with each dive lasting 20 minutes or so.

- **There are freshwater seals** in Lake Baikal in Russia.

◀ Seal pups (babies) like this one grow a thick, furry coat.

Moths

- **Like butterflies**, moths belong to the insect group Lepidoptera.

- **Most moths** have fat, hairy bodies, and feathery or thread-like antennae.

- **Many moths** fly at dusk or at night. By day, they rest on tree trunks and in leaf litter, where their drab color makes them hard for predators such as birds to spot.

- **Tiger moths** give out high-pitched clicks to warn that they taste bad and so escape being eaten.

- **The biggest moths** are the Hercules moth and the bent wing ghost moth, with wingspans of over 10in (20cm).

- **Night-flying** moths shiver their wings to warm them up for flight.

- **Hawk moths** are powerful fliers and migrate long distances. The oleander hawk moth flies from tropical Africa to far northern Europe in summer.

- **The caterpillars of small moths** live in seeds, fruit, stems, and leaves, eating them from the inside.

- **The caterpillars of big moths** feed on leaves from the outside, chewing chunks out of them.

- **When threatened**, the caterpillar of the puss moth rears up and thrusts its whip-like tail forward, and squirts a jet of formic acid from its head end.

- **Every caterpillar spins silk**, but the cloth silk comes from the caterpillar of the white *Bombyx mori* moth, known as the silkworm.

▶ Hawk moths have very long tongues for sucking nectar from flowers. They often hover like hummingbirds when feeding.

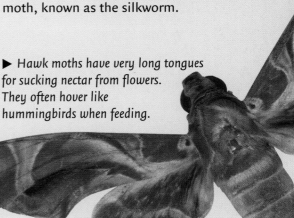

Bird eggs and nests

★ STAR FACT ★
Great auks' eggs are pointed at one end to stop them rolling off their cliff-edge nests.

- **All birds** begin life as eggs. Each species' egg is a slightly different color.

- **The plover's egg** is pear-shaped. The owl's is round.

- **Hornbills** lay just one egg a year. Partridges lay up to 20 eggs. Hens and some ducks can lay around 350 a year.

- **Most birds build nests** to lay their eggs in—usually bowl-shaped and made from twigs, grasses, and leaves.

- **The biggest nest** is that of the Australian mallee fowl, which builds a mound of soil 16ft (5m) across, with egg-chambers filled with rotting vegetation to keep it warm.

- **The weaverbirds** of Africa and Asia are very sociable. Some work together to weave huge, hanging nests out of straw, with scores of chambers. Each chamber is for a pair of birds and has its own entrance.

- **Ovenbirds** of Central and South America get their name because their nests look like clay ovens made by local people. Some ovenbirds' nests are 10ft (3m) high.

- **Flamingoes** nest on lakes, building mud nests that look like upturned sandcastles poking out of the water. They lay one or two eggs on top.

- **The great treeswift** lays its single egg in a nest the size of an eggcup.

▶ After they lay their eggs, most birds sit on them to keep their eggs warm until they are ready to hatch. This is called incubating the eggs.

Defense

- **Animals** have different ways of escaping predators—most mammals run away, while birds take to the air.

- **Some animals** use camouflage to hide (see Colors and markings). Many small animals hide in burrows.

- **Turtles and tortoises** hide inside their hard shells.

▼ Meerkats stand on their hind legs and give a shrill call to alert other meerkats to danger.

★ STAR FACT ★
The hognosed snake rolls over and plays dead to escape predators. It even smells dead.

- **Armadillos** curl up inside their flexible body armor.

- **The spiky-skinned** armadillo lizard of South Africa curls up and stuffs its tail in its mouth.

- **Hedgehogs**, porcupines, and echidnas are protected by sharp quills (spines).

- **Skunks** and the stinkpot turtle give off foul smells.

- **Plovers** pretend to be injured to lure hunters away from their young.

- **Many animals defend themselves** by frightening their enemies. Some, such as peacock butterflies, flash big eye-markings. Others, such as porcupine fish and great horned owls, blow themselves up much bigger.

- **Other animals** send out warning signals. Kangaroo rats and rabbits thump their feet. Birds shriek.

Gorillas and other apes

- **Apes** are our closest relatives in the animal world. The great apes are gorillas, chimpanzees, and the orangutan. Gibbons are called lesser apes.

- **Like us**, apes have long arms, and fingers and toes for gripping. They are smart and can use sticks and stones as tools.

- **Gorillas** are the biggest of all apes, weighing up to 500lb (225kg) and standing as tall as 6.5ft (2m). They are gentle vegetarians and eat leaves and shoots.

- **There are two gorilla species**, both from Africa: the eastern lowland and mountain gorilla and the western lowland.

- **Mountain gorillas** live in the mountains of Rwanda and Uganda. There are only about 650 of them.

- **When danger threatens a gorilla troop**, the leading adult male stands upright, pounds his hands against his chest, and bellows loudly.

- ◄ Gorillas climb trees only to sleep at night or to pull down branches to make a one-night nest on the ground. They usually walk on all fours.

- **Chimpanzees** are an ape species that live in the forests of central Africa.

- **Chimpanzees** are very clever and use tools more than any other animal apart from humans—they use leaves as sponges for soaking up water to drink, for example, and they crack nuts with stones.

- **Chimpanzees** communicate with each other through a huge range of grunts and screams. They also communicate by facial expressions and hand gestures, just as humans do. Experiments have shown that they can learn to respond to many words.

- **Only a few orangutans** remain in the forests of Borneo and Sumatra. They get their name from a local word for "old man of the woods."

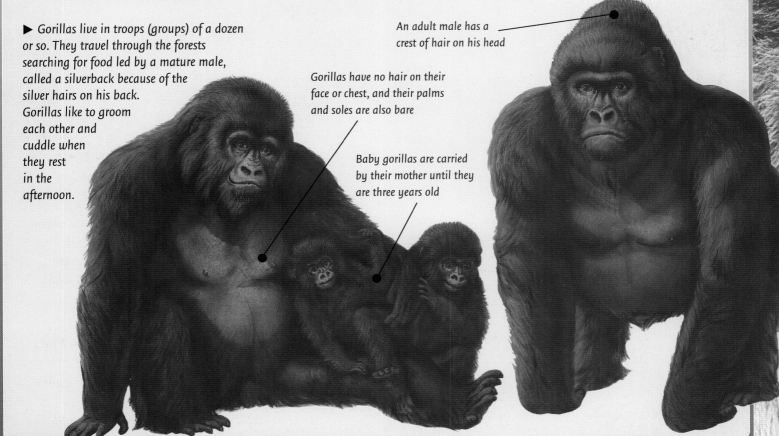

▶ Gorillas live in troops (groups) of a dozen or so. They travel through the forests searching for food led by a mature male, called a silverback because of the silver hairs on his back. Gorillas like to groom each other and cuddle when they rest in the afternoon.

An adult male has a crest of hair on his head

Gorillas have no hair on their face or chest, and their palms and soles are also bare

Baby gorillas are carried by their mother until they are three years old

Rhinos and hippos

- **Rhinoceroses** are big, tough-skinned animals of Africa and southern Asia.

- **Black and white** African rhinos and the smaller Sumatran rhino have two horns in the middle of their heads. Indian and Javan rhinos have just one.

- **Powdered rhino horn** is believed by some to be a love potion, so thousands of rhinos have been slaughtered and most kinds are now endangered.

- **Baluchitherium** lived 20 million years ago and was atype of rhino. At over 16.5ft (5m) tall, it was much bigger than any elephant.

◀ The African black rhino is almost extinct in the wild. Between two to three thousand are left on nature reserves.

- **Hippopotamuses** are big, gray, pig-like creatures that live in Africa. They have the biggest mouth of any land animal.

- **When a hippo yawns** its mouth gapes wide enough to swallow a sheep whole, but it only eats grass.

- **Hippos spend their days** wallowing in rivers and swamps, and only come out at night to feed.

- **A hippo's eyes**, ears, and nose are all on the top of its head, and so remain above the water when the rest of its body is completely submerged.

- **The word hippopotamus** comes from the Ancient Greek words for horse (hippo) and river (potamos).

> ★ STAR FACT ★
> The African white rhinoceros's horn can grow to over 5ft (1.5m) long.

Salmon

▲ Salmon returning to their spawning ground make mighty leaps up raging torrents. The journey can take months.

- **Salmon** are river and ocean fish caught or farmed in huge quantities for food.

- **All salmon** are born in rivers and lakes far inland, then swim downriver and out to the ocean.

- **Adult salmon** spend anything from six months to seven years in the oceans, before returning to rivers and swimming upstream to spawn (lay their eggs).

- **More than five salmon species**, including the sockeye and the chinook, spawn in zrivers running into the North Pacific.

- **Cherry salmon** spawn in eastern Asian rivers, and amago salmon spawn in Japanese rivers.

- **Atlantic salmon** spawn in rivers in northern Europe and eastern Canada.

- **Spawning salmon** return to the same stream where they were born, up to 2,000mi (3,000km) inland.

- **To reach their spawning grounds**, salmon have to swim upstream against strong currents, often leaping as high as 15ft (5m) to clear waterfalls.

- **When salmon** reach their spawning grounds, they mate. The female lays up to 20,000 eggs on gravel.

- **After spawning**, the weakened salmon head down river again, but few make it as far as the ocean.

Turtles and tortoises

- **Turtles and tortoises** are reptiles that live inside hard, armored shells. Along with terrapins, they make up a group called the chelonians.

- **Turtles** live in the ocean, freshwater or on land, tortoises live on land, and terrapins live in streams and lakes.

- **The shield** on the back of a chelonian is called a carapace. Its flat belly armor is called a plastron.

- **Most turtles and tortoises** eat plants and tiny animals. They have no teeth, just jaws with very sharp edges.

- **Tortoises** live mostly in hot, dry regions and will hibernate in winter if brought to a cold country.

- **Turtles and tortoises** live to a great age. One giant **tortoise** found in 1766 in Mauritius lived 152 years.

- **The giant tortoise** grows to as long as 5ft (1.5m).

> ★ STAR FACT ★
> Giant tortoises were once kept on ships to provide fresh meat on long voyages.

- **The leatherback turtle** grows to as long as 8ft (2.5m) and weighs more than 1,800lb (800kg).

- **Every three years**, green turtles gather together to swim thousands of miles to Ascension Island in the mid-Atlantic, where they lay their eggs ashore by moonlight at the highest tide. They bury the eggs in the sand, to be incubated by the heat of the sun.

▼ *Tortoises are very slow moving and placid.*

Antelopes and deer

- **Antelopes and deer** are four-legged, hooved animals. Along with cows, hippos, and pigs, they belong to the huge group called artiodactyls, animals with an even number of toes on each foot.

- **Antelopes and deer** chew the cud like cows, they chew food again, after first partially digesting it in a special stomach.

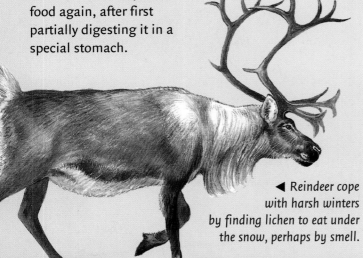

◄ *Reindeer cope with harsh winters by finding lichen to eat under the snow, perhaps by smell.*

- **Most antelope species live** in herds in Africa. Many are very graceful and also fast runners.

- **The horns** on an antelope's head last its lifetime.

- **Deer have branching antlers** of bone (not horn) on their heads, which drop off and grow again each year.

- **Most deer species live** in woods and grasslands in mild regions such as northern Europe and North America.

- **The moose or elk** can grow antlers more than 6.5ft (2m) wide.

- **Male deer** are called stags, young males are bucks, females are does, and babies are fawns.

- **Usually only stags** have antlers. The only female deer to have them are caribou or reindeer, which are the same species of deer but with different names.

> ★ STAR FACT ★
> Caribou can survive in the icy cold of Spitsbergen Island in the Arctic circle.

Evolution

▶ All life on Earth may have evolved almost 4 billion years ago from organisms like this archaebacteria. Archaebacteria thrive in extreme conditions such as those on the early Earth. This one came from under the Antarctic ice. Others thrive in scorching undersea volcanic vents.

- **Charles Darwin's** *Theory of Evolution*, first published in 1859, showed how all species of plant and animal adapt and develop over millions of years. Only the fittest survive.

- **Darwin's theory** depended on the fact that no two living things are alike.

- **Some animals** start life with characteristics that give them a better chance of surviving to pass the characteristics on to their offspring.

- **Other animals' characteristics** mean that they are less likely to survive.

- **Over many generations** and thousands of years, better-adapted animals and plants survive and flourish, while others die out or find a new home.

- **Fossil discoveries** since Darwin's time have supported his theory, and lines of evolution can be traced for thousands of species.

- **Fossils** also show that evolution is not always as slow and steady as Darwin thought. Some scientists believe change comes in rapid bursts, separated by long slow periods when

little changes. Other scientists believe that bursts of rapid change interrupt periods of long steady change.

- **For the first 3 billion years** of Earth's history, the only life forms were microscopic, single-celled, marine (sea) organisms such as bacteria and amoeba. Sponges and jellyfish, the first multi-celled creatures, appeared by 700 million years ago (mya).

- **About 600 mya**, evolution speeded up dramatically in what is called the Precambrian explosion. Thousands of different organisms appeared within a very short space of time, including the first proper animals with bones and shells.

- **After the Precambrian**, life evolved rapidly. Fish developed, then insects and then, about 380 mya, amphibians—the first large creatures to crawl on land. About 340 mya, reptiles evolved— the first large creatures to live entirely on land.

- **Dinosaurs** developed from these early reptiles about 220 mya and dominated the Earth for 160 million years. Birds also evolved from the reptile and cynodonts—furry, mammal-like creatures.

Hyracotherium

Mesohippus

Parahippus

Merychippus

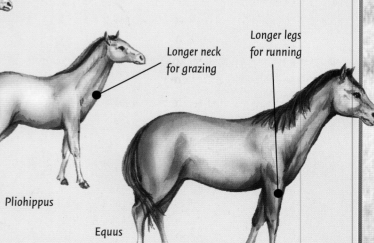

Pliohippus

Equus

Longer neck for grazing

Longer legs for running

▶ The gradual evolution of the horse shows how creatures adapt to changing conditions over million years. One of the horse's earliest ancestors, Hyracotherium, appeared about 45 mya. It was a small woodland creature which browsed on leaves and was suited to the widespread woodlands of the time. So was mesohippus. But from then on, the woods began to disappear and grasslands became more widespread—and it paid to be bigger to run fast to escape predators. The modern horse, Equus, is the latest result of evolutionary adaptation.

What are insects?

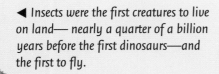

◄ *Insects were the first creatures to live on land— nearly a quarter of a billion years before the first dinosaurs—and the first to fly.*

- **Insects** may be tiny, but there are more of them than all the other animals put together— over 1 million known species.

- **They range** from tiny flies to huge beetles, and they are found everywhere there is land.

- **Insects** have six legs and a body divided into three sections—which is why they are called insects ("in sections"). The sections are the head, thorax (middle), and abdomen.

- **An insect's body** is encased in such a tough shell (its exoskeleton) that there is no need for bones.

- **Insect grow** by getting rid of their old exoskeleton and replacing it with a bigger one. This is called molting.

- **Some insects change** dramatically as they grow. Butterflies, moths, and beetles undergo metamorphosis (see Butterflies). Grasshoppers and mayflies begin as wingless nymphs, then gradually grow wings with each molt. Silverfish and springtails simply get bigger with each molt.

- **Insects' eyes** are called compound because they are made up of many lenses—from six (worker ants) to more than 30,000 (dragonflies).

- **Insects have** two antennae (feelers) on their heads.

- **Insects** do not have lungs. Instead, they breathe through holes in their sides called spiracles, linked to their body through tubes called tracheae.

- **The world's longest insect** is the giant stick insect of Indonesia, which can grow to 13in (33cm) long.

Woodpeckers and toucans

- **Woodpeckers** are closely related to the colorful toucans and jacamars of tropical rain forests.

- **Woodpeckers**, toucans, barbets, jacamars, and honeyguides all have two toes on each foot pointing forward and two pointing backward.

- **Woodpeckers** use their powerful bills to bore into tree trunks to get at insects. They spear the insects with their incredibly long tongues.

- **Gila woodpeckers** escape desert heat by nesting inside giant saguaro cacti (here it can be 86°F/30°C cooler).

- **Redheaded woodpeckers** drill holes in trees and use them to store acorns for winter, wedging them in very tightly so that squirrels cannot steal them.

- **Woodpeckers** claim their territory not by singing, but

▲ *The toucan's giant beak is full of air holes, so it is not heavy enough to overbalance the bird. Toucans eat mainly small fruit.*

by hammering their bills against trees.

- **Honeyguides** lead honey badgers to bees' nests. The badger opens them to get the honey and the bird gets beeswax.

- **When toucans sleep**, they turn their heads around and lay their bills down their backs.

> ★ **STAR FACT** ★
> At 9in (23cm), the toucan's bill is much longer than its body.

Mice and rats

▶ *Rabbits and hares look like rodents but they belong to another group of mammals called lagomorphs or "leaping shapes."*

- **Mice and rats** belong to a group of 1,800 species of small mammals called rodents. The group also includes voles, lemmings, squirrels, beavers, porcupines, and guinea pigs.

- **All rodents** have two pairs of razor-sharp front teeth for gnawing nuts and berries, and a set of ridged teeth in their cheeks for chewing.

- **A rodent's front teeth**, called incisors, grow all the time. Only gnawing keeps them the same length.

- **Rats and mice** are by far the most common rodents—they have adapted well to living alongside humans.

- **Brown and black rats** carry germs for diseases such as food poisoning, plague, and typhus.

- **Hares** live above ground and escape enemies through sheer speed. Rabbits live in burrows underground.

- **Baby hares** are born above ground, covered in fur, and with their eyes open. Rabbits are born naked and blind in burrows.

- **Rabbits breed quickly**—a female can have 20 babies every month during the breeding season, and her babies will have their own families after six months.

- **One rabbit** could have more than 33 million offspring in three years, if they all survived to breed.

- **A single mouse** can produce up to 34 young in one litter.

▶ *Rats and mice have long thin tails, pointed noses, beady black eyes and four very sharp front teeth.*

Ducks and geese

- **Ducks, geese, and swans** are known as waterfowl, and they all live on or near freshwater.

- **Waterfowl** can float for hours and have webbed feet for paddling along. On water they are graceful, but on land they waddle awkwardly, since their legs are set far back under their body for swimming.

- **Ducks** have shorter necks and wings, and flatter bills than swans. Male ducks are called drakes, and females, ducks. Babies are called ducklings.

◀ *Canada geese breed in the far north of Canada and Alaska, and migrate south to warmer regions in the fall.*

- **Diving ducks** (such as the pochard, tufted duck, and the scoter) dive for food such as roots, shellfish, and insects on the river bed.

- **Dabbling ducks** (such as the mallard, widgeon, gadwall, and the teal) dabble—they sift water through their beaks for food.

- **Some dabblers** lap water at the surface. Others up-end, sticking their heads into the water to sift out water weeds and snails from muddy water.

- **Swans** are the largest waterfowl. They have long elegant necks and pure white plumage, apart from the black-neck swan of South America and the Australian black swan.

- **Baby swans** are called cygnets and are mottled gray.

- **Geese** mostly graze on grass. Unlike ducks, which quack and swans which hiss, geese honk.

- **Baby geese** are called goslings.

Coral reef fish

- **Many fish species** live in warm seas around coral reefs. They are often very colorful, which makes them instantly recognizable to their own kind.

- **Butterfly fish and angelfish** have slender, oval bodies and are popular as aquarium fish.

- **Male triggerfish** boost their color to attract females.

- **Cuckoo wrasse** are all born female, but big females change sex when they are between 7 and 13 years old.

- **Cleaner fish** are the health clinics of the oceans. Larger fish such as groupers line up for cleaner fish to go over them, nibbling away pests and dead skin.

- **The banded coral shrimp** cleans up pests in the same way as cleaner fish do, from fish such as moray eels.

- **The saber-toothed blenny** looks so like a cleaner fish it can

▲ Coral reefs are home to many brilliantly colored fish.

swim in close to big fish but then takes a bite out of them.

- **Cheilinus** is a carnivorous fish of coral reefs which changes color to mimic harmless plant-eating fish, such as parrotfish and goatfish. It swims alongside them, camouflaged, until it is close to its prey.

> ★ STAR FACT ★
> Cleaner fish will go to work inside a shark's mouth.

Ants and termites

- **Ants** are a vast group of insects related to bees and wasps. Most ants have a tiny waist and are wingless.

- **Ants** are the main insects in tropical forests, living in colonies of anything from 20 to millions.

- **Ant colonies** are all female. Most species have one or several queens which lay the eggs. Hundreds of soldier ants guard the queen, while smaller workers build the nest and care for the young.

- **Males** only enter the nest to mate with young queens, then die.

- **Wood ants** squirt acid from their abdomen to kill enemies.

- **Army ants** march in huge swarms, eating most small creatures they meet.

▲ African termites use mud and saliva to build amazing nests more than 40ft (12m) high, housing over 5 million termites.

- **Groups of army ants** cut any large prey they catch into pieces which they carry back to the nest. Army ants can carry 50 times their own weight.

- **Ants known as slavemakers** raid the nests of other ants and steal their young to raise as slaves.

- **Termite colonies** are even more complex than ant ones. They have a large king and queen who mate, as well as soldiers to guard them and workers to do all the work.

- **Termite nests** are mounds built like cities with many chambers, including a garden used for growing fungus. Many are air-conditioned with special chimneys.

Swifts and hummingbirds

- **Swifts and hummingbirds** are on the wing so much that their feet have become weak. This is why they are called *Apodiformes*, meaning "footless ones."

- **Swifts** are fast flying birds. Spine-tailed swifts of eastern Asia have been recorded at 150mph (240km/h).

- **Swifts use** their short, gaping bills to catch insects on the wing.

- **Swifts may fly** through the night without landing. They may even sleep on the wing. European swifts fly all the way to Africa and back without stopping.

- **When swifts land**, they cling to vertical surfaces such as walls, cliffs, and trees.

- **Great dusky swifts** nest and roost behind waterfalls, and have to fly through the water to get in and out.

> ★ **STAR FACT** ★
> To hover, horned sungem hummingbirds beat their wings 90 times per second.

▲ *Hummingbirds have long bills to suck nectar from flowers.*

- **Hummingbirds** are about 325 species of tiny, colorful, tropical birds which sip nectar from flowers.

- **Hummingbirds** are the most amazing aerial acrobats, hovering and twisting in front of flowers.

- **The bee hummingbird** is the world's smallest bird, including its long bill, it measures just 2in (5cm).

Lemurs and lorises

- **Lemurs** are small furry creatures with long tails and big eyes. They are primates, like monkeys and humans.

- **Lemurs** live only on the islands of Madagascar and Comoros, off the east coast of Africa.

- **Most lemurs** are active at night but the ring-tailed lemur lives mostly on the ground and is active by day.

▲ *Ring-tailed lemurs get their name from their black-ringed tail which they raise to show where they are.*

- **Lemurs** eat fruit, leaves, insects, and small birds.

- **The ring-tailed lemur** rubs its rear on trees to leave a scent trail for other lemurs to follow.

- **In the mating season**, ring-tailed lemurs have stink fights for females, rubbing their wrists and tails in stink glands under their arms and rear, then waving them at rivals to drive them off.

- **Lorises and pottos** are furry, big-eyed primates of the forests of Asia and Africa. All are excellent climbers.

- **Bushbabies** get their name because their cries sound like a human baby crying.

- **Bushbabies** are nocturnal animals and their big eyes help them see in the dark. Their hearing is so sensitive they have to block their ears to sleep during the day.

- **Tarsiers** of the Philippines are tiny, huge-eyed primates which look like cuddly goblins. They have very long fingers and can turn their heads halfway round to look backward.

Pythons and boas

- **Constrictors** are snakes that squeeze their victims to death, rather than poisoning them. They include pythons, boas, and anacondas.

- **A constrictor** does not crush its victim. Instead, it winds itself around, gradually tightening its coils until the victim suffocates.

- **Constrictors usually swallow** victims whole, then spend days digesting them. They have special jaws that allow their mouths to open very wide. A large meal can be seen as a lump moving down the body.

- **Pythons** are big snakes that live in Asia, Indonesia, and Africa. In captivity, reticulated pythons grow to 30ft (9m). Boas and anacondas are the big constrictors of South America.

- **Boas** capture their prey by lying in wait, hiding motionless under trees, and waiting for victims to pass by. But like all snakes, they can go for many weeks without eating.

- **Like many snakes**, most constrictors begin life as eggs. Unusually for snakes, female pythons take care of their eggs until they hatch by coiling around them. Even more unusually, Indian and green tree pythons actually keep their eggs warm by shivering.

- **Female boas** do not lay eggs, giving birth to live young.

- **Boas** have tiny remnants of back legs, called spurs, which males use to tickle females during mating.

- **Anacondas** spend much of their lives in swampy ground or shallow water, lying in wait for victims to come and drink. One anaconda was seen to swallow a 6ft (2m) long caiman (a kind of crocodile).

- **When frightened**, the royal python of Africa coils itself into a tight ball, which is why it is sometimes called the ball python. Rubber boas do the same, but hide their heads and stick their tails out aggressively to fool attackers.

▲ Pythons are tropical snakes that live in moist forests in Asia and Africa. They are the world's biggest snakes, rivaled only by giant anacondas. Pythons are one long tube of muscle, well able to squeeze even big victims to death. They usually eat animals about the size of domestic cats, but occasionally they go for really big meals such as wild pigs and deer.

★ STAR FACT ★
A 12–15ft (4–5m) long African rock python was once seen to swallow an entire impala (a kind of antelope) whole—horns and all.

Snails and slugs

- **Snails and slugs** are small, slimy, soft-bodied crawling creatures. They belong to a huge group of animals called mollusks which have no skeleton. Squid and oysters are also mollusks.

- **Snails and slugs** are gastropods, a group that also includes whelks and winkles.

- **Gastropod** means "stomach foot," because these animals seem to slide along on their stomachs.

- **Most gastropods** live in the ocean. They include limpets which stick firmly to shore rocks.

◀ Garden snails have a shell which they seal themselves into in dry weather, making a kind of trapdoor to save moisture. They have eyes on their horns.

- **Most land snails and slugs** ooze a trail of sticky slime to help them move along the ground.

- **Garden snails** are often hermaphrodites, which means they have both male and female sex organs.

- **The great gray slugs** of western Europe court by circling each other for over an hour on a branch, then launching themselves into the air to hang from a long trail of mucus. They then mate for 7 to 24 hours.

- **Among the largest gastropods** are the tropical tritons, whose 18in (45cm) shells are sometimes used as warhorns.

- **Some cone snails** in the Pacific and Indian oceans have teeth that can inject a poison which can actually kill people.

★ STAR FACT ★
Snails are a great delicacy in France, where they are called *escargot*.

Life in tropical rain forests

- **Tropical rain forests** are the richest and most diverse of all animal habitats.

- **Most animals** in tropical rain forests live in the canopy (treetops), and are either agile climbers or can fly.

- **Canopy animals** include flying creatures such as bats, birds, and insects, and climbers such as monkeys, sloths, lizards, and snakes.

▲ Year-round rainfall and warm temperatures make rain forests incredibly lush, with a rich variety of plant life.

- **Many rain forest creatures** can glide through the treetops: these include gliding geckos and other lizards, flying squirrels, and even flying frogs.

- **Some tree frogs** live in the cups of rainwater held by plants growing high up in trees.

- **Antelopes, deer, hogs, tapir** and many different kinds of rodent (see Mice and rats) roam the forest floor, hunting for seeds, roots, leaves, and fruit.

- **Beside rivers** in Southeast Asian rain forests, there may be rhinoceroses, crocodiles, and even elephants.

- **Millions of insect species** live in rain forests, including butterflies, moths, bees, termites, and ants. There are also many spiders.

- **Rain-forest butterflies and moths** are often big or vividly colored, including the shimmering blue morpho of Brazil and the birdwing butterflies.

- **Rain-forest birds** can be vividly colored too, and include parrots, toucans, and birds of paradise.

Sharks

- **Sharks** are the most fearsome predatory fish of the seas. There are 375 species, living mostly in warm seas.
- **Sharks** have a skeleton made of rubbery cartilage—most other kinds of fish have bony skeletons.
- **The world's biggest fish** is the whale shark, which can grow to over 40ft (12m) long. Unlike other sharks, the whale shark and the basking shark (at 30ft/9m long) mostly eat plankton and are completely harmless.

> ★ STAR FACT ★
> Great white sharks are the biggest meat-eating sharks, growing to over 23ft (7m) long.

- **A shark's main weapons** are its teeth – they are powerful enough to bite through plate steel.
- **Sharks** put so much strain on their teeth that they always have three or four spare rows of teeth in reserve.
- **Nurse sharks** grow a new set of teeth every eight days.
- **Up to 20** people die from recorded shark attacks yearly.
- **The killing machine** of the shark world is the great white shark, responsible for most attacks on humans.
- **Hammerhead sharks** can also be dangerous. They have T-shaped heads, with eyes and nostrils at the end of the T.

◀ A shark's torpedo-shaped body makes it a very fast swimmer.

Dinosaurs

- **Dinosaurs** were reptiles that dominated life on land from about 220 million to 65 million years ago, when all of them mysteriously became extinct.
- **Although modern reptiles** walk with bent legs splayed out, dinosaurs had straight legs under their bodies: this meant they could run fast or grow heavy.
- **Some dinosaurs** ran on their back two legs, as birds do. Others had four sturdy legs like an elephant's.
- **Dinosaurs** are split into two groups according to their hipbones. Saurischians had reptile-like hips and ornithischians had bird-like hips.
- **Saurischians** were either swift, two-legged predators called theropods, or hefty four-legged herbivores called sauropods.
- **Theropods** had acute eyesight, fearsome claws, and sharp teeth. They included Tyrannosaurus rex, one of the biggest hunting animals to ever live on land, over 50ft (15m) long, 15ft (5m) tall.

- **Sauropods** had massive bodies, long tails, and long, snake-like necks.
- **The sauropod Brachiosaurus** was more than 75ft (23m) long, weighed 80 tons and was 40ft (12m) tall. It was one of the biggest creatures ever to live on land.
- **Most dinosaurs** are known from fossilized bones, but fossilized eggs, footprints, and droppings have also been found.
- **Some scientists** think the dinosaurs died out after a huge meteor struck the Earth off Mexico, throwing up a cloud that blocked the Sun's light and heat.

▶ Dinosaur means "terrible lizard," and they came in all shapes and sizes. This is a plant-eating sauropod called Diplodocus.

Pandas

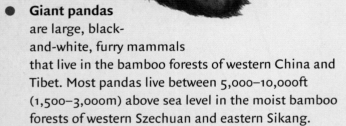

▶ Giant pandas are big, chubby animals, usually weighing well over 220lb (100kg). When they stand on their hind legs they are as tall as a man. But pandas have inefficient digestive systems and to sustain their huge bulk they have to eat more continuously than most other animals.

An extra thumb helps pandas to hold the bamboo while they are chewing

Giant pandas eat only a certain kind of bamboo

● **Giant pandas** are large, black-and-white, furry mammals that live in the bamboo forests of western China and Tibet. Most pandas live between 5,000–10,000ft (1,500–3,000m) above sea level in the moist bamboo forests of western Szechuan and eastern Sikang.

● **Giant pandas are among the rarest species** of animal in the world. There are probably fewer than 1,000 left. The giant panda's habitat has been cut back by the loss of forests for wood and farmland.

● **One reason** that giant pandas are rare is because they feed only on the shoots of bamboos. Some of these bamboos flower once every century and then die, and it is many years before the seeds grow into new plants.

● **Giant pandas** spend most of their time sitting around on the ground eating, but they are surprisingly agile tree climbers.

● **Giant pandas spend 12 hours** a day feeding on bamboo shoots, because their digestive system is so ineffective that they have to eat more than 90lb (40kg) of bamboo a day.

● **To help it hold the bamboo**, the panda has an extra "thumb"—it is not really a thumb, but a bone on the wrist which is covered by a fleshy pad.

● **The red panda** is a much smaller animal than the giant panda and it sleeps in trees, curled up like a cat.

● **Red pandas** look a little like raccoons and people once thought that pandas were related to raccoons, even though giant pandas look more like bears. DNA tests have shown that red pandas are close to raccoons, but that giant pandas are closer to bears.

● **In the wild**, giant pandas give birth to one or two cubs a year. The cubs are very tiny and the mother has to give up eating to take care of them for the first ten days or so. The cubs usually stay with their mother for nearly one year.

● **Attempts to breed** pandas in zoos have largely failed. Washington Zoo's giant panda Ling Ling, for instance, gave birth to several cubs in the 1970s and 1980s, but the cubs died very soon after birth.

▶ Giant pandas look like clowns with their black eye patches and ears. No one knows quite what the purpose of these eye patches is. When giant pandas were first introduced to Europe in 1869 by French priest Père Armand David, many people believed they were hoaxes.

! NEWS FLASH !
Chinese zoologists hope to clone giant pandas to save them for the future.

Flies

▶ Flies have only one pair of real wings. The hind wings are small stumps called halteres which help a fly balance in flight.

- **Flies** are one of the biggest groups of insects, common nearly everywhere. There are over 90,000 species.

- **Unlike other insects**, flies have only one pair of real wings.

- **Flies** include bluebottles, black flies, gnats, horseflies, midges, mosquitoes, and tsetse flies.

- **A house fly** flies at more than 4mph (7km/h)—equal to flying 350,000 times its own length in an hour. If a jumbo jet flew at the same speed relative to its length for an hour, it would get almost right around the world.

- **Alaskan flies** can stand being frozen at temperatures of −75°F (−60°C) and still survive.

- **Flies suck up** their food, typically sap from rotting plants and fruit. Houseflies often suck liquids from manure. Blowflies drink from rotting meat.

- **The larvae (young) of flies** are called maggots, and they are tiny, white, wriggling tube-shapes.

- **Flies resemble or mimic** many other kinds of insects. There are wasp flies, beetle flies, ant flies, and moth flies.

- **Many species** of fly are carriers of dangerous diseases. When a fly bites or makes contact, it can infect people with some of the germs it carries—especially the flies that suck blood. Mosquitoes spread malaria, and tsetse flies spread sleeping sickness.

> ★ STAR FACT ★
> The buzzing of a fly is the sound of its wings beating. Midges beat their wings 1,000 times a second.

Sparrows and starlings

- **More than 70 percent** of all bird species—over 5,000 species altogether—are perching birds, or Passerines. They have feet with three toes pointing forward and one backward, to help them cling to a perch.

- **Perching birds** build neat, small, cup-shaped nests.

- **Perching birds sing**, this means that their call is not a single sound, but a sequence of musical notes.

- **Songbirds**, such as thrushes, warblers, and nightingales, are perching birds with especially attractive songs.

- **Usually only male songbirds** sing—and mainly in the mating season, to warn off rivals and attract females.

- **Sparrows** are small, plump birds, whose chirruping song is familiar almost everywhere.

- **Starlings** are very common perching birds which often gather in huge flocks, either to feed or to roost.

- **All the millions** of European starlings in North America are descended from 100 set free in New York's Central Park in the 1890s.

▲ Starlings often gather on overhead cables ready to migrate.

- **Many perching birds**, including mynahs, are talented mimics. The lyre bird of southeastern Australia can imitate car sirens and chainsaws, as well as other birds.

- **The red-billed quelea** of Africa is the world's most abundant bird. There are over 1.5 billion of them.

Spiders

- **Spiders** are small scurrying creatures which, unlike insects, have eight legs not six, and bodies with two parts not three.
- **Spiders** belong to a group of 70,000 creatures called arachnids, which includes scorpions, mites, and ticks.
- **Spiders** live in nooks and crannies almost everywhere in the world, especially if there is plenty of vegetation to feed them.
- **Spiders are hunters** and most of them feed mainly on insects. Despite their name, bird-eating spiders rarely eat birds, preferring lizards and small rodents, such as mice.

▲ Like all arachnids, spiders have eight legs, plus two "arms" called pedipalps and a pair of fangs called chelicerae. They also have eight simple eyes.

- **Spiders have eight eyes**, but most have poor eyesight and hunt by feeling vibrations with their legs.
- **Many spiders** catch their prey by weaving silken nets called webs. Some webs are simple tubes in holes. Others, called orb webs, are elaborate and round. Spiders' webs are sticky to trap insects.
- **The Australian trapdoor** spider ambushes its prey from a burrow with a camouflaged entrance flap.
- **Most spiders** have a poisonous bite which they use to stun or kill their prey. Tarantulas and sun spiders crush their victims with their powerful jaws.
- **The bite of black widow, redback** and funnel-web spiders is so poisonous that it can kill humans.

Cockles and mussels

- **Cockles and mussels** belong to a group of mollusks called bivalves, which includes oysters, clams, scallops, and razorshells.
- **Bivalve** means "having two valves," and all these creatures have two halves to their shells, joined by a hinge that opens like a locket.
- **Most bivalves feed** by filtering food out from the water through a tube called a siphon.
- **Cockles** burrow in sand and mud on the shore. Mussels cling to rocks and breakwaters between the high and low tide marks.
- **Oysters** and some other mollusks line their shells with a hard, shiny, silvery white substance called nacre.
- **When a lump of grit** gets into an oyster shell, it is gradually covered in a ball of nacre, making a pearl.

- **The best pearls** come from the Pinctada pearl oysters that live in the Pacific Ocean. The world's biggest pearl was nearly 5in (12cm) across and weighed 14lb (6.4kg). It came from a giant clam.
- **Scallops** can swim away from danger by opening and shutting their shells rapidly to pump out water. But most bivalves escape danger by shutting themselves up inside their shells.
- **A giant clam** found on the Great Barrier Reef was over 3ft (1m) across and weighed more than 0.25 tons.
- **There are colonies** of giant clams living many thousands of feet down under the oceans, near hot volcanic vents.

◀ There are two main kinds of seashell: univalves like these (which are a single shell), and bivalves (which come in two, hinged halves).

Reptiles and amphibians

- **Reptiles** are scaly-skinned animals which live in many different habitats mainly in warm regions. They include crocodiles, lizards, snakes, and tortoises.

- **Reptiles are cold-blooded**, but this does not mean that their blood is cold. A reptile's body cannot keep its blood warm, and it has to control its temperature by moving between hot and cool places.

- **Reptiles bask in the sun** to gain energy to hunt, and are often less active at cooler times of year.

- **A reptile's skin** looks slimy, but it is quite dry. It keeps in moisture so well that reptiles can survive in deserts. The skin often turns darker to absorb the sun's heat.

- **Although reptiles grow** for most of their lives, their skin does not, so they must slough (shed) it every now and then.

> ★ STAR FACT ★
> Reptiles were the first large creatures to live entirely on land, over 350 million years ago.

▶ Like all reptiles, crocodiles rely on basking in the sun to gain energy for hunting. At night, or when it is cold, they usually sleep.

- **Amphibians** are animals that live both on land and in water. They include frogs, toads, newts, and salamanders.

- **Most reptiles** lay their eggs on land, but amphibians hatch out in water as tadpoles, from huge clutches of eggs called spawn.

- **Like fish**, tadpoles have gills to breathe in water, but they soon metamorphose (change), growing legs and lungs.

- **Amphibians** never stray far from water.

Pets

▲ Pit bulls terriers were first bred from bulldogs and terriers as fighting dogs, by miners in the 18th century.

- **There are over 500 breeds** of domestic dog. All are descended from the wolves first tamed 12,000 years ago to help humans hunt. Dogs have kept some wolf-like traits such as guarding territory and hiding bones.

- **Many pet dogs** were originally working dogs. Collies were sheepdogs. Terriers, setters, pointers, and retrievers all get their names from their roles as hunting dogs.

- **The heaviest dog breed** is the St. Bernard, at more than 200lb (90kg). The lightest is the miniature Yorkshire terrier, under 11lb (500g).

- **Cocker spaniels** were named because they were used by hunters to flush out woodcocks in the 14th century.

- **Chihuahuas** were named after a place in Mexico—the Aztecs thought them sacred.

- **The first domestic cats** were wild African bushcats tamed by the Ancient Egyptians to catch mice 3,500 years ago.

- **Like their wild ancestors**, domestic cats are deadly hunters, agile, with sharp eyes and claws, and often catch mice and birds.

- **Cats spend** a great deal of time sleeping, in short naps, but can be awake and ready for action in an instant.

- **Tabby cats** get their name from Attab in Baghdad (now in Iraq), where striped silk was made in the Middle Ages.

- **A female cat** is called a queen. A group of cats is called a clowder. A female dog is a bitch. A group of dogs is a kennel.

- **All pet golden hamsters** are descended from a single litter which was discovered in Syria in 1930.

Fleas and lice

- **Fleas and lice** are small wingless insects that live on birds and mammals, including humans. Dogs, cats, and rats are especially prone to fleas.

- **Fleas and sucking lice** suck their host's blood.

- **Chewing lice** chew on their host's skin and hair or feathers. Chewing lice do not live on humans.

- **Fleas and lice** are often too small to see easily. But adult fleas grow to over 0.1in (2mm) long.

- **A flea** can jump 1ft (30cm) in the air—the equivalent of a human leaping 650ft (200m) in the air.

- **The fleas** in flea circuses perform tricks such as jumping through hoops and pulling wagons.

- **Fleas spread** by jumping from one animal to another, to suck their blood.

> ★ STAR FACT ★
> Fleas jump with a force of 5oz (140g): over 20 times that required to launch a space rocket.

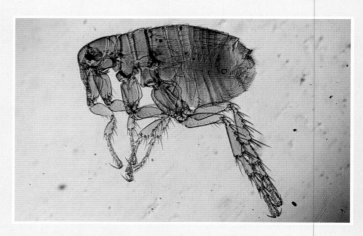

▲ A much-magnified flea with its powerful back legs for jumping.

- **When fleas lay their eggs**, they hatch as larvae and crawl off into the host's bedding, where they spin cocoons and emerge as adults two weeks later.

- **Head lice** gum their nits (eggs) to hair and spread from head to head through sharing of combs and hats.

Life in woodlands

- **Woodlands** in temperate zones between the tropics and the poles are home to many creatures.

- **Deciduous trees** lose their leaves in the fall. Evergreens keep theirs through cold winters.

- **In the leaf litter** under the trees live tiny creatures such as worms, millipedes, and ants and other insects.

▲ On a walk through a deciduous wood, you may be lucky enough to catch a glimpse of a shy young red deer as it crosses a clearing.

- **Spiders, shrews, salamanders, and mice** feed on the small creatures in the leaf litter.

- **Some birds**, such as woodcocks, nest on the woodland floor and have mottled plumage to hide themselvess.

- **Birds such as owls**, nuthatches, treecreepers, tits, woodpeckers, and warblers live on and in trees, as well as insects such as beetles, moths, and butterflies, and small mammals such as squirrels and raccoons.

- **Other woodland mammals** include badgers, chipmunks, opossums, stoats, weasels, polecats, pinemartins, and foxes.

- **Beavers, frogs, muskrats, and otters** live near woodland streams.

- **The few large woodland mammals** include bears, deer, wolves, and wild boar. Many of these have become rare because woods have been cleared away.

- **In winter**, many birds of deciduous woods migrate south, while small mammals like dormice hibernate.

Tigers

- **Tigers** are the largest of the big cats, with huge heads. The average male tiger's body grows to over 6.5ft (2m) long, plus a 3ft (1m) long tail.

- **Tigers live** in the forests of Asia, Sumatra, and Java, but as hunters kill them for their skin and farmers clear the forest for land, they are becoming very rare. They now live only on special reserves.

- **Tigers prey on large animals** such as deer, buffalo, antelopes, and wild pigs. They hunt silently at night, stalking their prey, then making a sudden bound.

- **A tiger is fast and strong** but tires quickly, and it will give up if it fails to catch its prey the first time.

- **Adult tigers** usually live alone, and males try to keep other males out of their territory. But when two tigers meet, they may rub one another's head in greeting.

- **A male tiger's territory** often includes that of two or three females. But they only meet to mate.

- **Tigers mark** out their territory by scratching trees and urinating on them.

- **Usually, two to four cubs** are born at a time. The cubs are playful and boisterous, and are totally dependent on their mother for 2 to 3 years.

▲ When a tiger roars, the sound can be heard for 2.5–3mi (4–5km) through the forest.

- **A tiger's stripes** make it instantly recognizable, but they make good camouflage in long grass and under trees. Each tiger has its own unique pattern of stripes.

- **White tigers** are rare. They have blue eyes, and their stripes are brown and white, not black and gold.

Most tigers have yellow eyes

In between the black stripes, the coat is amber or yellow

▼ Tigers are forest dwellers and can climb trees, but most of the time they like to lie around. On hot days, they will often lie in rivers to cool off and, unusually for a cat, they can swim quite well.

The fur on the throat, belly, and the insides of the legs is whitish

Male tigers usually have a ruff of hair around the face

Vultures

- **Vultures and condors** are the biggest birds of prey. They do not hunt, but feed on carrion (dead animals).

- **The palmnut vulture** is the only vegetarian bird of prey, and it feeds on oil nuts.

- **Many vultures are bald**, with no head feathers to mat with blood when digging into corpses.

- **The seven species** of New World vulture (those that live in the Americas) have a nostril hole right through their beak.

- **The Californian condor** is very rare. All the wild ones were captured in the mid 1980s, but some have since been bred in captivity and returned to the wild.

- **Vultures** are great fliers and spend hours soaring, scanning the ground for corpses with sharp eyes.

> ★ **STAR FACT** ★
> The Andean condor is the biggest flying bird,
> with a wingspan of 10ft (3m) or more.

▲ *A vulture closes in to feed on a dead animal.*

- **Condors** have such a sharp sense of smell that they can pinpoint a corpse under a thick forest canopy.

- **Vultures** have such weak bills that flesh must be rotten before they can eat it.

- **The lammergeier** is known as the bearded vulture because it has a beard of black bristles on its chin.

Strange sea creatures

- **Deepsea anglerfish** live deep down in the ocean where it is pitch black. They lure prey into their mouths using a special, fishing rod-like fin spine with a light at its tip.

- **Anglerfish** cannot find each other easily in the dark, so when a male meets a female he stays with her until mating time.

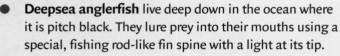

- **Hatchet fish** have giant eyeballs that point upward so they see prey from below as silhouettes against the surface.

- **Viperfish** shine in the dark, thousands of feet down, and look like a jet airliner at night, with rows of lights along their bodies.

◄ *If threatened, the dragon fish will try to stab its attacker with its poisonous spines.*

- **Siphonophores** are colonies of tiny creatures that live in the deep oceans. They string themselves together in lines 65ft (20m) long and glow, so they look like Christmas tree lights.

- **The cirrate octopod** looks like jello because its skin is 95 percent water—the water cannot be crushed by the intense pressure of the deep oceans where it lives.

- **The weedy seadragon** of Australia is a seahorse, but it looks just like a piece of flapping seaweed.

- **The sleeper shark** lives in the freezing depths of the North Atlantic and Arctic oceans. It is 20ft (6.5m) long, but very slow and sluggish.

- **Flashlight fish** have light organs made by billions of bacteria which shine like headlights. The fish can suddenly block off these lights and change direction in the dark to confuse predators.

- **In the Arab–Israeli War** of 1967 a shoal of flashlight fish was mistaken for enemy frogmen and blown right out of the water.

Baby animals

- **All baby mammals** except monotremes (see Strange mammals) are born from their mother's body, but most other creatures hatch from eggs.

- **Most creatures** hatch long after their parents have disappeared. Birds and mammals, though, usually look after their young.

- **Most birds** feed their hungry nestlings until they are big enough to find food themselves.

- **Some small birds** may make 10,000 trips to the nest to feed their young.

- **Cuckoos** lay their egg in the nest of another, smaller bird. The foster parents hatch it and take care of it as it grows. It then pushes its smaller, foster brothers and sisters out of the nest.

- **Mammals nurse** their young (they feed them on the mother's milk). The nursing period varies. It tends to be just a few weeks in small animals like mice, but several years in large animals like elephants.

- **Many animals** play when they are young. Playing helps them develop strength and co-ordination, and practice tasks they will have to do for real when adults.

- **When they are young**, baby opossums cling all over their mother as she moves around.

- **Some baby animals**, including baby shrews and elephants, go around in a long line behind the mother, clinging to the tail of the brother or sister in front.

▶ *Lion cubs are taken care of by several females until they are big enough to fend for themselves. Like many babies they have big paws, head and ears for their body.*

Chameleons

- **Chameleons** are 85 species of lizard, most of which live on the island of Madagascar and in mainland Africa.

- **The smallest chameleon**, the dwarf Brookesia, could balance on your little finger. The biggest, Oustalet's chameleon, is the size of a small cat.

- **A chameleon** can look forward and backward at the same time, as each of its amazing eyes can swivel in all directions independently of the other.

- **Chameleons** feed on insects and spiders, hunting them in trees by day.

- **A chameleon's tongue** is almost as long as its body, but is normally squashed up inside its mouth.

- **A chameleon shoots** out its tongue in a fraction of a second to trap its victim on a sticky pad at the tip.

- **The chameleon's tongue** is fired out from a special launching bone on its lower jaw.

- **Most lizards** can change color, but chameleons are experts, changing quickly to all sorts of colors.

▲ *Most of a chameleon's bulging eyes are protected by skin.*

- **Chameleons change color** when they are angry or frightened, too cold or too hot, or sick—but they change color less often to match their surroundings.

- **The color of the skin** is controlled by pigment cells called melanophores, which change color as they change size.

Life in cold regions

▲ *Other animals are the only substantial food in the Arctic wastes, so polar bears have to be carnivorous.*

- **The world's coldest places** are at the Poles in the Arctic and Antarctic, and high up mountains.
- **Only small animals** such as ice worms and insects can stand the extreme polar cold all year round.
- **Insects** such as springtails can live in temperatures as low as −36.4°F (−38°C) in Antarctica, because their body fluids contain substances that do not freeze easily.
- **Birds** such as penguins, snow petrels, and skuas live in Antarctica. So do the leopard seals that eat penguins.
- **Polar seas** are home to whales, fish, and shrimp-like krill.
- **Fish of cold seas** have body fluids that act like car anti-freeze to stop them from freezing.
- **Mammals such as polar bears**, sea lions, and walruses are so well insulated against the cold with their fur and fat that they can live on the Arctic ice much of the year.
- **Many animals** live on the icy tundra land in the far north of America and Asia. They include caribou, Arctic foxes and hares, and birds such as ptarmigans and snowy owls.
- **Arctic foxes and hares**, ermines, and ptarmigans turn white in winter to camouflage them against the snow.

★ STAR FACT ★
Ptarmigans can survive through the bitter Arctic winter by eating twigs.

Starfish and sea urchins

- **Despite their name** starfish are not fish, but belong instead to a group of small sea creatures called echinoderms.
- **Sea urchins** and sea cucumbers are also echinoderms.
- **Starfish** have star-shaped bodies and are predators that prey mostly on shellfish such as scallops and oysters. They have five strong arms which they use to prise open their victim. The starfish then inserts its stomach into its victim and sucks out its flesh.
- **Each arm** of a starfish has on the underside hundreds of tiny, tube-like "feet." Bigger tubes inside the starfish's body pump water in and out of the "feet," flexing the arms and driving the starfish along.
- **Starfish** often drop some of their arms off to escape an enemy, but the arms grow again.

◄ *Starfish that live in cooler water tend to be brown or yellow, whereas many tropical starfish can be bright red or even blue.*

- **Sea urchins** are ball-shaped creatures. Their shell is covered with bristling spines, which can be poisonous and up to 16in (40cm) long in some species.
- **A sea urchin's spines** are used for protection. Urchins also have sucker-like feet for moving.
- **A sea urchin's mouth** is a hole with five teeth, on the underside of its body.
- **Sea cucumbers** have no shell, but a leathery skin and a covering of chalky plates called spicules.
- **When threatened**, a sea cucumber throws out pieces of its gut as a decoy and swims away. It grows a new one later.

Dragonflies

- **Dragonflies** are big hunting insects with four large transparent wings, and a long slender body that may be a shimmering red, green, or blue.

- **Dragonflies have** 30,000 separate lenses in each of their compound eyes, giving them the sharpest vision of any insect.

- **A dragonfly** can see something that is stationary from almost 6ft (2m) away, and something moving two to three times farther away.

- **As it swoops** in on its prey, a dragonfly pulls its legs forward like a basket to scoop up its victim.

- **Dragonflies** often mate in mid-air, and the male may then stay hanging on to the female until she lays her eggs.

> ★ STAR FACT ★
> Dragonflies can reach speeds of almost 60mph (100km/h) to escape from birds.

- **Dragonfly eggs** are laid in water or in the stem of a water plant, and hatch in two to three weeks.

- **Newly hatched dragonflies** are called nymphs and look like fatter, wingless adults.

- **Dragonfly nymphs** are ferocious hunters, often feeding on young fish and tadpoles.

- **Dragonfly nymphs** grow and molt over a period of several years, before they climb on to a reed or rock to emerge as an adult.

▶ *Dragonflies are big insects even today, but hundreds of millions of years ago, there were dragonflies with wings that were well over 2.5ft (75cm) across.*

Owls

- **Owls** are nocturnal and hunt by night, unlike most other hunting birds.

- **There are two big families of owl:** barn owls and typical owls.

- **There are 135 species** of typical owl, including the great horned owl.

- **There are 12 species** of barn owl. The common barn owl is the most widespread, it is found on every continent but Antarctica.

◀ *An owl's big eyes face straight forward to focus on an object. However, owls cannot move their eyes and have to swivel their whole head to look to the side or the rear.*

- **Small owls** eat mostly insects. Bigger owls eat mice and shrews. Eagle owls can catch young deer.

- **In the country,** the tawny owl's diet is 90 percent small mammals, but many now live in towns where their diet is mainly small birds such as sparrows and starlings.

- **Owls have huge eyes** that allow them to see in almost pitch darkness.

- **An owl's hearing** is four times as sharp as a cat's.

- **An owl can pinpoint** sounds with astonishing accuracy from the slight difference in the sound levels it receives in each of its ears.

- **Most bird's eyes** look out to the sides, but an owl's look straight forward like a human's. This is probably why the owl has been a symbol of wisdom since ancient times.

- **The flight feathers** on an owl's wing muffle the sound of the bird's wingbeat so that it can swoop almost silently down on to its prey.

Turkeys and hens

- **Turkeys**, chickens, geese, and ducks are all kinds of poultry: farm birds bred to provide meat, eggs, and feathers.

- **Chickens** were first tamed 5,000 years ago, and there are now over 200 breeds, including bantams and Rhode Island reds.

- **Female chickens** and turkeys are called hens. Male chickens are called roosters or cockerels. Male turkeys are toms. Baby turkeys are poults.

- **To keep hens laying**, their eggs must be collected daily. If not, the hens will wait until they have a small

◄ Roosters are renowned for their noisy cries every morning as the sun rises. This harsh cry is called a crow.

clutch of eggs, then try to sit on them to hatch them.

- **Factory farm hens** spend their lives crowded into rows of boxes or cages inside buildings.

- **Free-range hens** are allowed to scratch outdoors for insects and seeds.

- **Chickens** raised only for eating are called broilers.

- **Turkeys** are a kind of pheasant. There are several species, but all are descended from the native wild turkey of North America, first tamed by Native Americans 1,000 years ago.

- **Male turkeys** have a loose fold of bare, floppy skin called a wattle hanging down from their head and neck.

> ★ STAR FACT ★
> All domestic chickens are descended from the wild red jungle fowl of India.

Strange mammals

- **The duck-billed platypus** and the echidnas live in Australia and are the only monotremes—mammals that lay eggs.

- **Duck-billed platypuses** are strange in other ways, too. They have a snout shaped like a duck's bill and webbed feet, which is why they are so happy in water.

▼ The Tasmanian devil may be small, but it can be very fierce.

- **Platypuses hatch** from eggs in a river-bank burrow.

- **Platypus babies** lick the milk that oozes out over the fur of their mother's belly.

- **Echidnas** are also known as spiny anteaters because they are covered in spines and eat ants.

- **After a female echidna** lays her single egg, she keeps it in a pouch on her body until it hatches.

- **The Tasmanian devil** is a small, fierce, Australian marsupial (see Kangaroos and koalas). It hunts at night and eats almost any meat, dead or alive.

- **Tasmanian devils** stuff their victims into their mouth with their front feet.

- **The sugar glider** is a tiny, mouse-like jungle marsupial which can glide for 150ft (45m) between trees.

- **The aardvark** is a strange South African mammal with a long snout and huge claws. It can shovel as fast as a mechanical digger to make a home or find ants.

What is a fish?

- **Fish** are slim, streamlined animals that live in water. Many are covered in tiny shiny plates called scales. Most have bony skeletons and a backbone.

- **There are well over 21,000 species** of fish, ranging in length from 0.5in (8mm) to 40ft (12m).

▼ *Angling (catching fish) is a popular pastime all around the world. The fish is hooked as it bites the lure or bait.*

★ **STAR FACT** ★
The drum fish makes a drumming sound with its swim bladder.

- **Fish** are cold-blooded.

- **Fish breathe** through gills, rows of feathery brushes inside each side of the fish's head.

- **To get oxygen**, fish gulp water in through their mouths and draw it over their gills.

- **Fish** have fins for swimming, not limbs.

- **Most fish** have a pectoral fin behind each gill and two pelvic fins below to the rear, as well as a dorsal fin on top of their body, an anal fin beneath, and a caudal (tail) fin.

- **Fish let gas in** and out of their swim bladders to float at particular depths.

- **Some fish** communicate by making sounds with their swim bladder. Catfish use them like bagpipes.

Worms

- **Worms** are long, wriggling, tube-like animals. Annelids are worms such as the earthworm whose bodies are divided into segments.

- **There are 15,000 species** of annelid. Most live underground in tunnels, or in the ocean.

- **The largest earthworm** is the giant earthworm of South Africa, it can be as long as 7yd (6.5m) when extended.

- **Earthworms** spend their lives burrowing through soil. Soil goes in the mouth end, passes through the gut, and comes out at the tail end.

- **An earthworm** is both male and female (called a hermaphrodite), and after two earthworms mate, both develop eggs.

- **Over half the annelid species** are marine (ocean) bristleworms, such as ragworms and lugworms. They are named because they are covered in bristles, which they use to paddle over the seabed or dig into the mud.

- **The sea mouse** is a furry-haired bristleworm.

- **Flatworms** look like ribbons or as though an annelid worm has been ironed flat. Their bodies do not have real segments. Many flatworms live in the ocean or in ponds.

- **Flukes** are flatworms that live as parasites inside other animals. Diseases like bilharzia are caused by flukes.

- **Tapeworms** are parisitic flatworms that live inside their host's gut and eat their food.

▶ *Earthworms aerate soil as they burrow in it, mixing up layers and making it more fertile with their droppings.*

INDEX

Acknowledgments

Artist: Jim Channell

The publishers would like to thank the following sources for the photographs used in this book:

Page 6 (B/R) Corbis; Page 19 (B/R) Corbis; Page 27 (B/R) Corbis; Page 42 (T/C) Science photo library.

All other photographs are from MKP Archives

Instant
Immersion ™

French

developed and written by Mary March, M.A.

Instant Immersion™

developed and written by Mary March, M.A.

ISBN 1-59150-309-4

Edited by Naty de Menezes
Creative Director: Tricia Vander Leest
Illustrations by Elizabeth Haidle
Art Director: Paul Haidle
Design by Paul Haidle
Maps by Lonely Planet®

Printed on 100% recycled paper. Printed in the U.S.A.

TABLE OF CONTENTS

INTRODUCTION

Bienvenue (welcome) to *Instant Immersion French*™! An understanding of other cultures is critical in becoming part of a larger global community. Knowing how to communicate in other languages is one way to facilitate this process. You have chosen a truly global language to learn. There are diverse francophone (French–speaking) cultures in Europe, Canada, Africa, and the Caribbean, having a worldwide influence on cuisine, fashion, dance, theatre, architecture, and arts. French is also the official working language of many international organizations and is the second language used on the Internet.

Now let's get down to learning some French. Did you know that close to half of all English vocabulary has roots in the French language? This means you already know the meaning of many French words such as: *radio, courage, police, concert, train, possible,* and *restaurant.* Other French words look very much like their English equivalents: *musique, banane, nationalité, bicyclette, hôpital, ordinaire, and lettre.* You just have to learn the pronunciation. (And you will see that learning French pronunciation is not as difficult as you might think!)

This book will help you learn the basics of communicating in French in a way that will be fun and easy for you. We include many popular phrases and expressions and show you how these are used in real life through example conversations and stories. Our book also provides an easy pronunciation system that will give you the confidence you need to speak French. A wide range of interesting and valuable topics give you a firm grounding in the language, including how to order food like a local, how to travel comfortably within the country, even what to do when things go 'wrong'.

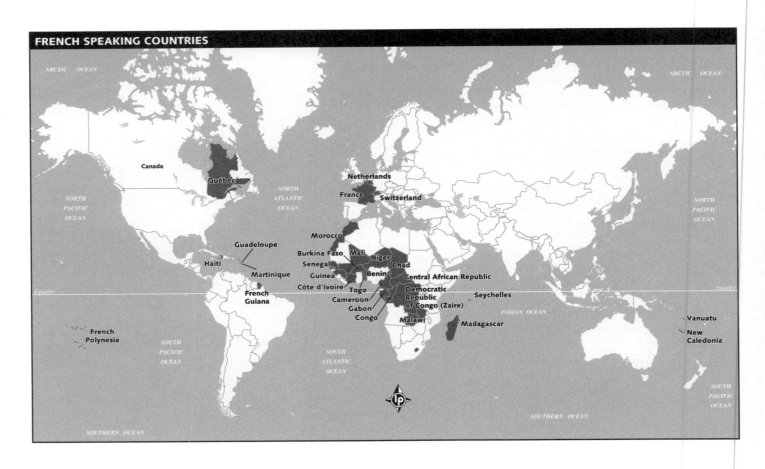

FRENCH SPEAKING COUNTRIES

PRONUNCIATION GUIDE

VOWELS

Paying particular attention to the four accent marks used on some of the vowels will help you learn the sounds that correspond with them. Yes, it does make a difference in which direction the accent mark points! Note: See chapter 2 for an explanation of nasal vowels.

French Letters	Symbol	English/French Examples
a, à, â	ah	ahh/papa *(pah-pah)*
é, er, ez	ay	day/bébé *(bay-bay)*
et	ay	et *(ay)*
ai	ay	j'ai *(zhay)*
ê, è	eh	pet/mère *(mehr)*
e + 2 consonants	eh	belle *(behl)*
et, ei, ai	eh	ballet *(bah-leh)*, seize *(sehz)*/mais *(meh)*
e,	uh	the/le *(luh)*/prenez *(pruh-nay)*
eu	uh	peu *(puh)*, jeune *(zhuhn)*
i, y,	ee	meet/midi *(mee-dee)*, Sylvie *(seel-vee)*
ill, ail, eil	y	yes/famille *(fah-mee-y)*, travail *(trah-vahy)*, soleil *(soh-lehy)*
ill	eel	eel/ville *(veel)*, village *(vee-lahzh)*,
o, ô, au, eau	o	boat/mot *(moh)*, hôtel *(o-tehl)*, aussi *(o-see)*, beau *(bo)*
o	oh	love/homme *(ohm)*, téléphone *(tay-lay-fohn)*
ou, où, oû	oo	youth/douze *(dooz)*, beaucoup *(bo-coo)*
oy, oi	wah	wash/moi *(mwah)*
u	ew*	tu *(tew)*, salut *(sah-lew)*

*This sound does not exist in English. It is not difficult to pronounce, but it does take some practice. Try this: Put your lips in the position of saying oo (as in "moo"), but say ee (as in "me").

CONSONANTS

Most French consonants sound like they do in English. Here are some of the consonants and corresponding symbols you will see in this book:

ch	sh	chocolat *(shoh-koh-lah)*, chaud *(sho)*
g (before e, i, y)	zh	(like the S in "measure"), âge *(ahzh)*,
gn	ny	(like the "n" in "onion"), montagne *(mohN-tah-nyuh)*
j	zh	(like the S in "measure"), Jacques *(zhahk)*

Important! Beware that most consonants at the end of a word are not pronounced. In the word "restaurant" (rehs-to-rahN), for example, the final "n" and "t" are not pronounced, and in plurals, the final "s" is not pronounced: hôtels (o-tehl). (Note also that "h" is always silent.) Only c, r, f, and l (the consonants in the word "careful") are usually pronounced at the end of words.

The French "r" will also need some practice to get it right. If you can gargle, then you can produce this sound. Try to say "Sara" making the "r" way back in your throat. Let your tongue rest on the bottom of your mouth when you say the French "r".

This book has 16 chapters. You can work through the book chapter by chapter or skip around to the topics that most interest you. Study the expressions and vocabulary before reading the dialog or story. Say them out loud to practice your pronunciation. Read through the dialog or story as many times as you need in order to understand it. Then read it out loud. Check your answers to the exercises in the Answer Key at the back of the book. Finally, get in a French mood! Put on a beret, drink French wine, put on an Edith Piaf tape, buy a baguette, speak English with a French accent, whatever it takes....
Amusez-vous bien! (Have fun!)

CHAPTER 1

(bohN-zhoor)
Bonjour!
Good morning!

Baseball. Parking. Titanic. Taxi. Madonna. Now say each of those words with the stress on the last syllable. *Voilà (vwah-LAH)*! You have a French accent. Putting a slight stress on the last syllable of words is a general rule in French that is good to keep in mind. Whenever you come across a French word with more than one syllable, just remember to put that stress on the final syllable.

You should also know that people who speak French like to link (or connect) their words. If you read this sentence "I ate an egg at eight" linking the words together, it would sound like this: *"I yay-ta-neg-ga-teight"*. This is what happens a lot in French when words begin with vowels and one reason why it is often difficult to pick out individual words when you hear the language. You will know when you need to connect the words as you read the pronunciation above the words in each chapter. The following expressions are examples of linking words together.

(sah meh tay-gahl)
Ça m'est égal.
It's all the same to me.

(ohN nyee-vah)
On y va!
Let's go!

VOCABULARY

(eel)
il
he

(unuhm)
un homme
man

(luh ma-taN)
le matin
morning

(el)
elle
she

(ewn fahm)
une femme
woman

(pahr-lay)
parler
to speak

(boN-zhoor)
Bonjour.
Good morning.

(sah vah)
Ça va?
How are you?

(sah vah beeyahN)
Ça va bien.
I'm fine.

(twa)
toi (familiar)
you

(vuh)
veux
want

(ah-lay)
aller
to go

(praNdr)
prendre
to take
(but with food or meals, it means "to have")

(mahN-zhay)
manger
to eat

(luh day-zhuh-nay)
le déjeuner
lunch

(luh deenay)
le dîner
dinner

(luh puh-tee day-zhuh-nay)
le petit déjeuner
breakfast

DIALOG

(seh luh ma-taN) (ewn fahm)   (Leez)   (ay unN nohm) (Pol) (pahrl)
C'est le matin. Une femme (Lise) et un homme (Paul) parlent.
it is   and   are speaking

(bohN-zhoor)   (sah vah)
Lise: "Bonjour Paul. Ça va?"

(ay twa)
Paul: "Bonjour, Lise. Ça va bien. Et toi?"
and you?

(oo vuh tew praNdr luh puh-tee day-zhuh-nay)
Lise: "Ça va. Où veux–tu prendre le petit déjeuner?"
where do you want to have

(sa meh tay-gahl) (ohN puh ah-lay o kah-fay duh lo-tehl)
Paul: "Ça m'est égal. On peut aller au café de l'hôtel."
we can   to the   of the

(zhuh vuh mahN-zhay uhN krwa-sahN)
"Je veux manger un croissant."
I want to eat a crescent-shaped bread.

(mwa-ohsee) (ahlor, oh Nyee-vah)
Lise: "Moi aussi. Alors, On y va!"
me too   then

PRACTICE

le petit déjeuner	le dîner	veux	prendre
le déjeuner	où	tu	aller

Fill in the blanks using words from the box above.

1. Où _____ prendre _____ ? *(8 pm)*

2. Où veux–tu _____ ? *(12:00 noon)*

3. _____ veux–tu prendre _____ ? *(8 am)*

4. _____ veux–tu aller?

MATCHING

Match the sentence with the picture.

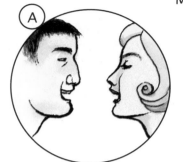

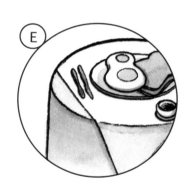

_____ 1. Où veux-tu prendre le petit déjeuner?

_____ 2. Une femme et un homme parlent.

_____ 3. Je veux manger.

_____ 4. C'est le matin.

_____ 5. Ça m'est égal.

_____ 6. Alors, on y va!

FOCUS

SUBJECT PRONOUNS

Singular			Plural		
je	*(zhuh)*	I	nous	*(noo)*	we
tu	*(tew)*	you (familiar)	vous	*(voo)*	you (familiar)
vous	*(voo)*	you (formal)	vous	*(voo)*	you (formal)
il	*(eel)*	he, it (m)	ils	*(eel)*	they (m)
elle	*(ehl)*	she, it (f)	elles	*(ehl)*	they (f)
on	*(ohN)*	one, we			

VERB FOCUS

(zhuh mahN zhuN puh)
Je mange un peu.
I eat a little.

(mahN-zhay)
manger
to eat

(noo mahN-zhoN bo-koo)
Nous mangeons beaucoup.
We eat a lot.

(tew mahNzh duh lah veeyaNd)
Tu manges de la viande.
You eat meat.
(singular/informal)

(voo mahN-zhay day paht)
Vous mangez des pâtes.
You eat pasta.
(plural and singular/informal)

(ehl mahNzh dahN lah vwa-tewr)
Elle mange dans la voiture.
She eats in the car.

(eel mahNzh sewr lah plahzh)
Elles mangent sur la plage.
They (female) eat on the beach.

(eel mahNzh sewr lah plahzh)
Il mange sur la plage.
He eats on the beach.

(eel mahNzh o lee)
Ils mangent au lit.
They (male) eat in bed.

NOTES

Tu or *vous?* The French use *tu* when talking to a relative, friend, child or animal. Teenagers use *tu* with each other even when they first meet. If a person older than you asks you to *tutoyer*, he/she is not asking you to dance, but is in fact giving you permission to use *tu* (informal) rather than *vous* (formal) when speaking to that person. In order to avoid being impolite, it's best to begin using *vous* with people when you first meet.

On means "one" in the sense of "people": *Ici on parle français.* (People speak French here.) Important: In spoken French, *on* is widely used instead of *nous*. *Nous parlons français = On parle français.* (We speak French.) Be careful to use the third person singular form of the verb.

(prahNdr)
PRENDRE
to take

je prends	*(zhuh prahN)*	*I take*
tu prends	*(tew prahN)*	*you take*
il, elle, on prend	*(eel, ehl, ohN prahN)*	*he, she one takes*
nous prenons	*(noo pruh-nohN)*	*we take*
vous prenez	*(voo pruh-nay)*	*you take*
ils, elles prennent	*(eel, ehl prehn)*	*they take*

Here are some common expressions with *prendre*:

(ohn vah prahNdr luh pe-tee day-zhuh-nay)
On va prendre le petit déjeuner.
We are going to have breakfast.

(zhuh prahN luh traN)
Je prends le train.
I'm taking the train.

(tew vuh prahN druhN vehr)
Tu veux prendre un verre?
Do you want to have a drink?

CHAPTER 2

J'ai faim!
I'm hungry!

French is thought of as a "nasal" language because it has nasal vowels. Believe it or not, there are only 4 nasal vowels you have to learn in French. Look at the phrase *un bon vin blanc* (*uN bohN vaN blahNk* – a good white wine): There is an "n" in each word, which tells you that the vowel before it is a nasal vowel. Instead of pronouncing the "n", just try putting the preceding vowel in your nose. Pinch your nose and say "oh" (through your nose). Now put a "b" in front of the "oh" and you have said *bon*. (Remember... don't pronounce the "n".) Whenever you see an "n" or an "m" think "nose". Exception: two m's or n's together – *femme* (fahm), *homme* (ohm).

(kehl shahNs)
Quelle chance!
What luck!

(zhay faN)
J'ai faim!
I'm hungry!

VOCABULARY

(ahNtr)
entre
enter

(sor)
sort
leave

(kohN-tahN)
content
happy

(treest)
triste
sad

12

(ah-mee)
amie
female friend

(fro-mahzh)
fromage
cheese

(dun)
donne
give

NUMBERS

If you want to understand a room number, tell someone your phone number, or under-stand how much something is you are considering buying, you need numbers. Try to memorize the numbers 0–10 now. (Practice counting throughout the day!) More numbers will be introduced in later chapters.

0 *(zay-roh)* zéro

1 *(uhN)* un

2 *(duh)* deux

3 *(trwah)* trois

4 *(kahtr)* quatre

5 *(saNk)* cinq

6 *(sees)* six

7 *(set)* sept

8 *(weet)* huit

9 *(nuhf)* neuf

10 *(dees)* dix

NUMBER PRACTICE

Write the answers to these simple arithmetic problems in words.

1. trois + un = _____

2. six + quatre = _____

3. deux + trois = _____

4. huit – cinq = _____

5. neuf – huit = _____

6. dix – trois = _____

7. quatre x deux = _____

8. trois x trois = _____

STORY

(ahn ay sohN nah-mee zhew-lee sohN dahN zuhN kah-fay)
Anne et son amie Julie sont dans un café.
and her   are   in   a

(sahN-ndwee choh froh-mahzh)
Anne mange un sandwich au fromage.

(ah duh sahN-ndwee shoh froh-mahzh)
Julie a deux sandwichs au fromage.
has

(zhah kahNtr dahN luh kah-fay)
Jacques entre dans le café.
enters in the

(pray-zahNt)   (ah)   (ahN-shahN-tay dee zhahk)
Anne présente Jacques à Julie. "Enchanté", dit Jacques.
introduces   to   Pleased to meet you.

(pwee ahn dmahN dah zhahk seel ah faN)
Puis Anne demande à Jacques s'il a faim.
then   asks   if he is hungry

(eel ray-pohN wee zhay fahN)
Il répond "Oui, j'ai faim!"
yes

(lwee dohn uhN sahN-dweesh)
Julie lui donne un sandwich.
him

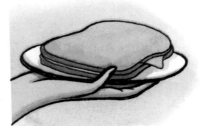

(mehr-see kehl shahNs)
"Merci. Quelle chance!" répond Jacques.
thank you

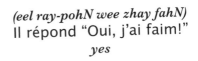

(ee lay treh kohN-tahN)   (dee zhuh voo zahn pree)
Il est très content. Julie lui dit "Je vous en prie."
is very   tells him you're welcome

PRACTICE

The statements below are all false. Change each one to make it true.

1. Anne et son amie mangent dans la voiture.

   _____

2. Julie a trois sandwichs. _____

3. Jacques sort du café. _____

4. Jacques est triste. _____

VERB FOCUS

| (ehtr) |
| être |
| *to be* |

(zhuh swee kohN-tahN(t)
Je suis content(e).
I am happy.

(tew eh kohN-tahN(t))
Tu es content.
You are happy.

(ehl eh kohN-tahNt)
Elle est contente.
She is happy.

(eel eh kohN-tahN)
Il est content.
He is happy.

(noo sohm treest)
Nous sommes tristes.
We are sad.

(voo zeht treest)
Vous êtes tristes.
You are sad.

(ehl sohN treest)
Elles sont tristes.
They (female) are sad.

(eel sohN treest)
Ils sont tristes.
They (male) are sad.

Here are some useful sentences with the verb "be":

(ehl eh dohk-tuhr/proh-feh-suhr/ahr-teest)
Elle est docteur/professeur/artiste.
She is a doctor/teacher/artist.

(lah vah-leez nwah reh tah mwah)
La valise noire est à moi.
The black suitcase is mine.

(shuh swee dah-kohr)
Je suis d'accord.
I agree.

(eel sohN tahN traN dmahN-zhay)
Ils sont en train de manger.
They are busy eating.

(oh neh tahN ruh-tahr)
On est en retard.
We are late.

CHAPTER 3

(Ehk-skew-zay mwah)
Excusez–moi!
Excuse me! Sorry!

If you are traveling to a foreign country, there will be many opportunities for you to start a conversation with native speakers of the language. Don't be shy! Of course some people will be in a hurry or won't want to talk to you. However, many people will be interested to meet someone traveling in their country. You'll want to learn some basic questions and appropriate responses as well as some useful expressions.

(zhay swahf)
J'ai soif.
I'm thirsty.

(zhuh swee fah-tee-gay)
Je suis fatigué.
I'm tired.

(suh neh pah grahv)
Ce n'est pas grave.
That's OK. Don't worry about it.
It's not serious.

VOCABULARY

(wee)
oui
yes

(duh)
de (d')
from

(oo)
où
where

(vyaN)
viens
come

(pahrl)
parle
speak

(uhN puh)
un peu
a little

(zhuh mah-pehl)
je m'appelle
my name is

(vwah-see)
voici
here is

USEFUL EXPRESSIONS

Here are some ways to say yes and no:

(wee)
OUI!
yes

(nohN)
NON!
no

(seh sa)
C'est ça!
That's right!

(meh wee)
Mais oui!
Certainly!

(byaN sewr)
Bien sûr!
Sure! Of course!

(ah nohN)
Ah, non!
No way!

(meh nohN)
Mais non!
Of course not!

(o kohN trehr)
Au contraire!
On the contrary!

17

Sometimes bumping into people by accident can lead to introductions and even friendships. Read what *Dan et Sylvie* have to say to each other after they bump into one another on the street.

Dan Duncan: l'homme   **Sylvie Simonet:** la femme   **Sophie:** la fille   *(luh gahr-sohN)*
David: le garçon

1 | **Dan:**   Excusez-moi!   **Sylvie:** Ce n'est pas grave.

2 | **Dan:**   *(voo zeht frahN-sehz)*
Vous êtes française?   **Sylvie:** Oui! D'où venez-vous?   *(doo vuh-nay voo)*
Are you French?

Dan: Je viens de Seattle, Washington.   *(kohN-mahN voo zah-play voo)*
Je m'appelle Dan Duncan. Et vous?   Comment vous appelez-vous?

3 | **Sylvie:** Je m'appelle Sylvie Simonet.   *(zhuh voo pray-zahNt mah fee-y)*
Je vous présente ma fille, Sophie.

4 | **Dan:**   *(sah-lew)*   *(keh lahzh ah-tew)*
Salut, Sophie. Quel âge as-tu?   **Sophie:** J'ai 8 ans.

5 | **Dan:**   *(mohN fees)*
Voici mon fils, David. Il parle un peu français.

Sophie: Bonjour, David. Quel âge as-tu?

6 | **David:** J'ai 5 ans et j'ai faim et j'ai soif et suis fatigué.

N O T E :   Notice the use of *"tu"* with the boy and girl and *"vous"* with the adult. Look back at Chapter 1 for the explanation of this rule.

PRACTICE

Study the dialog. Then, see if you can write the missing question. The response is given.

1. _____ ? J'ai 10 ans.

2. _____ ? Je viens de Boston.

3. _____ ? Je m'appelle Sylvie Simonet.

4. _____ ? Oui! Je suis américain.

*Note: A woman would say *Je suis américaine (zhuh swee zah-may-ree-kehn)*. A French woman says *Je suis française (zhuh swee frahN-sehz)*. A French man says *Je suis français (frahN-seh)*. A woman from *Québec (kay-behk)*: *Je suis québécoise (kay-bay-kwaz)*. A man from *Québec*: *Je suis québécois (kay-bay-kwah)*.

ASKING QUESTIONS IN FRENCH

A. The easiest way to ask a question in French is to simply raise your voice at the end of a sentence.

(voo zeht frahN-sehz)
Vous êtes française?
You're French?

(ay voo)
Et vous?
And you?

B. Another way is to invert the subject and the verb. (Put the pronoun after the verb.)

(doo vuh-nay voo)
D'où venez–vous?
Where do you come from?

(kohN-mahN voo zah-play voo)
Comment vous appelez–vous?
What's your name?

(keh lahzh ah-tew)
Quel âge as–tu?
How old are you?

C. Still another way is to put *Est-ce que (ehs-kuh)* "Is it that" at the beginning of the sentence. The order of the words stays the same.

(ehs kuh voo zeht fah-tee-gay)
Est–ce que vous êtes fatigué?
Are you tired?

(ehs kuh zhuh mahzh tro)
Est–ce que je mange trop?
Do I eat/am I eating too much?

PRACTICE

Now practice asking questions. Write a question using the method indicated (A, B, or C), putting the words in the correct order.

Ex: <u>français</u> /parlez/vous (A)

(voo pahr-lay frahN seh)
<u>Vous parlez français?</u> _____ ?

1. êtes/vous/français (C) _____ ?

2. faim/tu/as (A) _____ ?

3. avez/faim/vous (C) _____ ?

4. venez/d'où/vous (B) _____ ?

5. vous/mangez/les escargots (B) _____ ?

6. vous/quel âge/avez (A) _____ ?

```
                        AVOIR
                        to have

    j'ai                (zhay)                  I have
    tu as               (tew ah)                you have
    il, elle, on a      (eel, ehl, ohN ah)      he, she, one has
    nous avons          (noo zah-vohN)          we have
    vous avez           (voo zah-vay)           you have
    ils, elles ont      (eel, ehl zohN)         they have
```

Notice that many expressions in French with *avoir* + noun are expressed in English with be + adjective:

"I am thirsty" becomes *J'ai soif* (I have thirst).

Notice also that the French use *avoir* to state their age:

J'ai 10 ans rather than "I am 10 years old." However... *Je SUIS fatigué.*

Here are some other useful expressions with the verb *"avoir"*:

(zhay buh-zwaN duh)   *(tewah duh lah shahNs)*   *(zhay puhr)*
J'ai besoin de...   Tu as de la chance.   J'ai peur.
I need...   *You're lucky.*   *I'm afraid.*

(voo zah-vay reh-zohN)   *(zhay soh-mehy)*   *(voo zah-vay tohr)*
Vous avez raison.   J'ai sommeil.   Vous avez tort.
You're right.   *I'm sleepy.*   *You're wrong.*

```
                        PARLER
                        to speak

    je parle             (zhuh pahrl)           I speak
    tu parles            (tew pahrl)            you speak
    il, elle, on parle   (eel, ehl ohN pahrl)   he, she, one speaks
                                                (we speak)
    nous parlons         (noo pahr-lohN)        we speak
    vous parlez          (voo pahr-lay)         you speak
    ils, elles parlent   (eel, ehl pahrl)       they speak
```

CHAPTER 4

(kohN-byaN sa koot)
Combien ça coûte?
How much is it?

VOCABULARY

(keh-skuh)
Qu'est–ce que
what

(meh)
mais
but

(dahN)
dans
in

(da-kohr)
D'accord!
OK! Agreed!

(vwah-lah)
voilà
There you are. There it is.

(plew)
plus
more

(lahN-tmahN)
lentement
slowly

(ewn boo-lahN zhree)
une boulangerie
a bakery

(kohN-prahN)
comprends
understand

(voo-dreh)
voudrais
would like

(ewn boo-tehy do mee-nay-rahl)
une bouteille d'eau minérale
a bottle of mineral water

BE POLITE

(swah poh-lee)
Sois poli!
Be polite!

(mehr-see byaN)   *(bo-koo)*
merci bien *or* merci beaucoup
thank you very much

(nohN mehr-see)
non, merci
no thank you

(seel voo pleh)
s'il vous plaît *(formal)*
please

(duh ryaN)
de rien *(informal)*
you're welcome

(zhuh voo zahN pree)
je vous en prie
you're welcome

(seel tuh pleh)
s'il te plaît *(informal)*
please

(nohN mehr-see)
non, merci
no thank you

(o ruh-vwahr)
au revoir
good bye

Note: *Madame (mah-dahm)* (Mrs.) is used for older women, whether they are married or not. *Mademoiselle (mah-dmwah-zehl)* (Miss, Ms) is used for younger women.

Monsieur (muh-syuh) is used for men. *Messieurs-dames (meh-syuh-dahm)* (ladies and gentlemen) is very commonly used in formal situations when one or more women and men are addressed.

These titles are used a great deal in formal conversations and without the names of the people, even if the names are known:

Bonjour, madame.   Au revoir, monsieur.

STORY

(eel eh dee zuhr dew mah-taN)
Il est dix heures du matin.

(ee-zah-beh lay zhahN sohN tah pah-ree)
Isabelle et Jean sont à Paris.

(frahN-sehs)
Isabelle est française.

(eh tah-meh-ree-kaN meh)
John est américain mais il parle un
               but

(frahN-seh) (eel sohN dahN zewn)
peu français. Ils sont dans une boulangerie.
           in

(vahN-duhz)   *(bohN-zhoor)*
Vendeuse: Bonjour, messieurs–dames.

Isabelle: Bonjour, madame.

John: Bonjour, madame.

(keh-skuh voo day-zee-ray)
Vendeuse: Qu'est–ce que vous désirez?
What do you want?

(zhuh voo-dreh ewn bah-geht seel-voo-pleh)
Isabelle: Je voudrais une baguette, s'il vous plaît.
             long loaf of bread

(ay voo)   *(muh-syuh)*
Vendeuse: Et vous, monsieur?

Qu'est–ce que vous désirez?

(zhuh nuh kohN-prahN pah pahr-lay plew)
John: Je ne comprends pas. Parlez plus
I don't understand   *speak*

lentement, s'il vous plaît.
slowly

(dah-kohr)
Vendeuse: D'accord. Qu'est–ce que vous désirez?
     ok
            (duh zay-klehr o shoh-koh-lah)
John: Je voudrais deux éclairs au chocolat, s'il vous plaît.

Vendeuse: *(vwah-lah)* Voilà.

Isabelle: *(voo zah-vay duh lo mee-nay-rahl)* Vous avez de l'eau minérale?

Vendeuse: *(byaN sewr)* Bien sûr, mademoiselle.
of course

(ewn boo-tehy) (do mee-nay-rahl) Voilà. Une bouteille d'eau minérale.

Isabelle: *(kohN-byaN sa koot)* Merci bien, madame. Combien ça coûte?

Vendeuse: *(trwa zyuh-ro)* Trois euros, s'il vous plaît.
euro

Isabelle: Voilà trois euros.

Vendeuse: Merci, mademoiselle.

John et Isabelle: *(o ruh-vwahr)* Au revoir, madame.

Vendeuse: Au revoir, messieurs–dames.

DO YOU UNDERSTAND?

Read the dialog carefully and see if you can answer these questions. Answer in French or English. Check your answers in the back of the book.

1. Who is French in this dialog? _____

2. Why doesn't John understand? _____

3. What does John want to buy? _____

4. Who asks for mineral water? _____

5. Where does this scene take place? _____

NUMERAUX 11 - 22

11	12	13	14	15	16
(ohNz)	*(dooz)*	*(trehz)*	*(kah-torze)*	*(kahz)*	*(sehz)*
onze	douze	treize	quatorze	quinze	seize

17	18	19	20	21	22
(dee-seht)	*(dee-zweet)*	*(dee-znuhf)*	*(vaN)*	*(vaN tay uhN)*	*(vaN-duh)*
dix–sept	dix–huit	dix–neuf	vingt	vingt et un	vingt–deux

WHAT WOULD YOU LIKE?

(keh-skuh voo day-zee-ray)
Qu'est-ce que vous désirez?
What would you like? or How can I help you?

Je voudrais is the polite (conditional) form of the verb *vouloir* "to want" and is commonly used, but it's always good to say "please" – *s'il vous plaît* at the beginning or end of the sentence too.

Write the numbers in words, just for practice. Say the numbers out loud as you write them. Then practice saying each sentence with *s'il vous plaît.* at the end.
For example: *Je voudrais deux éclairs au chocolat, s'il vous plaît.*

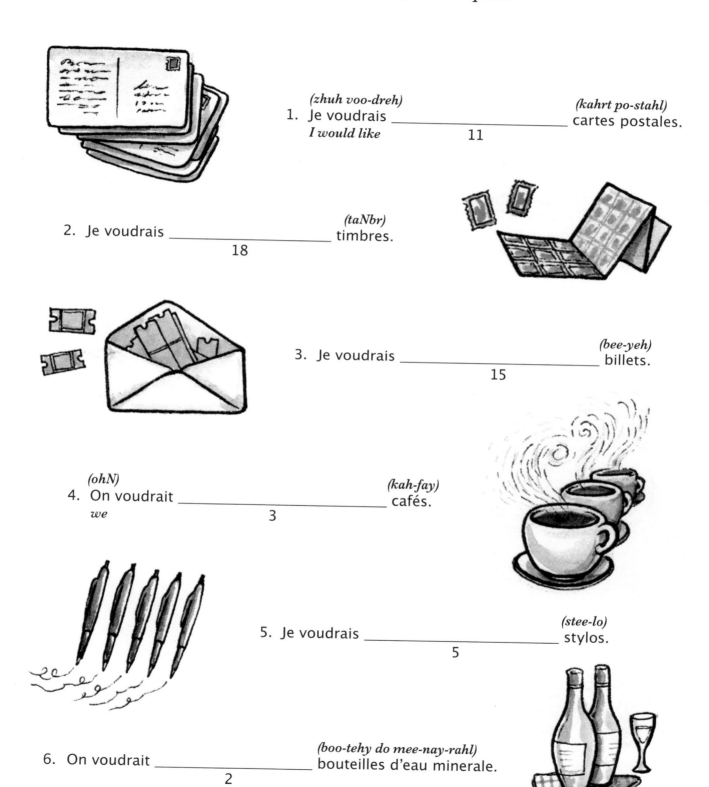

(zhuh voo-dreh)
1. Je voudrais _____ cartes postales.   *(kahrt po-stahl)*
   I would like   11

2. Je voudrais _____ timbres.   *(taNbr)*
                         18

3. Je voudrais _____ billets.   *(bee-yeh)*
                              15

(ohN)
4. On voudrait _____ cafés.   *(kah-fay)*
   we   3

5. Je voudrais _____ stylos.   *(stee-lo)*
                              5

6. On voudrait _____ bouteilles d'eau minerale.   *(boo-tehy do mee-nay-rahl)*
                         2

CHAPTER 5

(kehl zhoor sohm-noo)
Quel jour sommes–nous?
What day is it?

(luh koo duh foodr)
le coup de foudre
love at first sight

(lah fluhr)
la fleur
flower

(ahN-new-yuh/ahN-new-yuhz)
ennuyeux/ennuyeuse
boring

(too lay duh)
tous les deux
both

(ah-vwahr luh sahN sho)
avoir le sang chaud
to be quick-tempered

VOCABULARY

(luh zhar-daN)
le jardin
garden

(maN tnahN)
maintenant
now

(mah-rahN/mah-rahNt)
marrant/marrante
funny

(luh proh-grah-muhr)
le programmeur
computer programmer

(lah meh-zohN)
la maison
house

(lah vwa-tewr)
la voiture
car

(eh-may)
aimer
to like/love

(lay zyuh)
les yeux
eyes

(saN-pah-teek)
sympathique
nice

(lay-twahl)
l'étoile
star

FOCUS : VERBS

French verbs are either "regular", if the endings you add to the main part of the word follow a set pattern, or "irregular" if they don't.

There are three types of "regular" French verbs:

-er   (like *manger* – to eat and *parler* – to speak) These end in -er.

-ir   (like *finir* – to finish and *choisir* – to choose) These end in -ir.

-re   (like *vendre* – to sell and *attendre* – to wait for) These end in -re.

Most verbs in French are "regular", so all you have to do is learn the endings that go with the three different forms (-er, -ir, and -re) if you want to write them. If you only want to say them, it's even easier. In all regular verbs and in many irregular ones, the first three conjugations *(je, tu, il/elle/on)* are pronounced exactly the same. In the -er type, the *ils/elles* conjugation is also pronounced like the first three just mentioned.

Here is what to do if you want to conjugate *parler* or other verbs that end in -er: you just take off the -er, which leaves the stem *parl-*.
Now add the endings: *je, tu, il/elle/on: -e, -es, e*
                        nous, vous, ils/elles: -ons, -ez, -ent

This introductory book focuses on the –er verbs because it is the largest of the three types.
Warning! When you conjugate "manger", you must add an "e" to "nous mangeons" keeping the soft sound of the "g".

Here is an example of a regular -er verb conjugation:

(ah-bee-tay)
HABITER
to live

j'habite	*(zhah-beet)*	*I live*
tu habites	*(tew ah-beet)*	*you live*
il, elle, on habite	*(eel, ehl, ohN (n)ah-beet)*	*he, she, one lives*
nous habitons	*(noo zah-bee-tohN)*	*we live*
vous habitez	*(voo zah-bee-tay)*	*you live*
ils, elles habitent	*(eel, ehl zah-beet)*	*they live*

See page 32 for French colors.

(ah-laN ay mah-ree ah-bee tewn grahNd meh-zohN)
Alain et Marie habitent une grande maison bleue et rose.

(eel zohN tuhN puh-tee)　　*(day fluhr roo zheh zhon)*
Ils ont un petit jardin avec des fleurs rouges et jaunes.
they have

(eh)
Alain est programmeur.

(eel ah　ahN ay ah　lay zyuh vehr)
Il a 25 ans et a les yeux verts.
　　　has　　　　*green*

(treh　saN-pah-teek　meh)
Il est très sympathique, mais
　　very

(kehl-kuh-fwa eel a luh sahN sho)
quelquefois il a le sang chaud.
sometimes

(fahm dah-fehr)
Marie est une femme d'affaires.
　　　　businesswoman

(lay zyuh mah-rohN)
Elle a 26 ans et a les yeux marron.

Elle est marrante.

(poor tou lay duh)　　*(seh-teh luh koo)*
Pour tous les deux, c'etait le coup
for both of them　　　*it was love*

(duh foodr)
de foudre.
at first sight

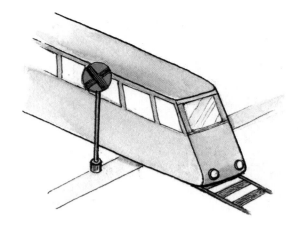

(too lay duh   sohn treh zoh-kew-pay)
Tous les deux sont très occupés.

(shahk   luhN-dee)   (vah)   (ahN traN)
Chaque lundi, Marie va à Paris en train.
each   Monday   goes to

(mehr-kruh-dee)   (vwah-tewr)
Chaque mercredi Alain va à Marseille en voiture.
each   Wednesday

(meh)   (vahN-druh-dee)   (mahN zhahN-sahNbl)
Mais chaque vendredi Alain et Marie mangent ensemble
but   Friday   together

(dahN luh reh-sto-rahN kee)   (lay-twahl roozh)
dans le restaurant qui s'appelle "L'Etoile Rouge".
which is called   the red star

PRACTICE

Complete the sentences in English or French (or both!). Use the vocabulary and the dialog to help you.

1. Alain and Marie live in a big blue and pink _____.

2. Alain is 25 _____.

3. Alain is very _____.

4. Marie is _____.

5. Alain doesn't like his _____.

6. Marie goes to Paris by _____.

7. Alain goes to Marseille by _____.

31

(blahN)
blanc
white

(bluh)
bleu
blue

(gree)
gris
gray

(mah-rohN)
marron
brown

(nwahr)
noir
black

(oh-rahNzh)
orange
orange

(zhon)
jaune
yellow

(vehr)
vert
green

(roz)
rose
pink

(roozh)
rouge
red

PRACTICE

(lay koo-luhr)
LES COULEURS

See how many colors you can remember.
Fill in the crossword puzzle with the French
words for the colors.

DOWN

1. yellow
2. blue
3. pink
4. orange
5. white

ACROSS

3. red
6. grey
7. brown
8. green

DAYS OF THE WEEK

(lay zhoor duh lah suh-mehn)
les jours de la semaine

Notice that the days of the week are not capitalized in French and they are all masculine. In addition, French calendars begin with Monday (not Sunday, like ours).

(luhN-dee)	*(mahr-dee)*	*(mehr-kruh-dee)*	*(zhuh-dee)*	*(vahN-druh-dee)*	*(sahm-dee)*	*(dee-mahNsh)*
lundi	mardi	mercredi	jeudi	vendredi	samedi	dimanche
Monday	*Tuesday*	*Wednesday*	*Thursday*	*Friday*	*Saturday*	*Sunday*

Find *les jours de la semaine* hidden in the puzzle. Then circle them.

u	a	c	x	w	s	c	s	l	i
i	d	e	r	d	n	e	v	s	d
i	d	n	u	l	m	p	x	a	u
v	n	r	c	z	g	p	g	m	e
d	i	m	a	n	c	h	e	e	j
q	c	s	c	m	q	u	a	d	i
m	e	r	c	r	e	d	i	i	r

PRACTICE

Put *les jours de la semaine* in order beginning with Monday by putting a number from 1 to 7 in front of each day.

_____ mercredi   _____ dimanche   _____ mardi   _____ vendredi

_____ lundi   _____ samedi   _____ jeudi

33

CHAPTER 6

(seh lwaN)
C'est loin?
Is it far?

Understanding directions in another language is particularly difficult, but not impossible! Of course it helps to have *une carte* (a map) so you can look at the names of the streets as the person you ask points to them. You don't have to understand every *mot* (word).

(fehr-may/fehr-may)
fermé/fermée
closed

(mahr-shay)
marchez
walk

(pruh-nay)
prenez
take

(oo-vehr/ouvehrt)
ouvert/ouverte
open

(seh proh-mnay)
se promener
to go for a walk

(preh duh)
près de
near

LISTEN FOR THE VERBS.
This will generally be the first word you hear because it will be in the command form: Walk, Take, Go, Turn, Go up, Go down, Cross.

LISTEN FOR THE DIRECTION WORDS.
right, left, straight ahead, next to, on the other side of, facing

LISTEN FOR THE NAMES OF THE STREETS.
These will be the hardest to understand. You can learn verbs and directions in advance, but names of people and places are more difficult because of the differences in pronunciation between English and French.

(lwaN)
loin
far

(mohN-tay)
montez
go up

(day-sahN-day)
descendez
go down

(leh pohN)
le pont
bridge

In Chapter 5 you learned how to conjugate "regular" verbs – those that have a set pattern of endings. The verb *aller* (to go) conjugated at the bottom of this page is an example of an "irregular" verb, (although since it ends in "er", it looks like a "regular verb). Since there is no pattern to the endings for "irregular" verbs, these forms must be memorized. Other examples of irregular verbs you have studied so far in this book are: *être* (to be), *avoir* (to have), and *prendre* (to take). (Although *prendre* looks like a regular -re verb, it has irregular endings in the plural forms: *prends, prends, prend, prenons, prenez, prennent.*) Try to memorize *aller*. It's a very useful verb! Just say them out loud in the order given in the box from the top (beginning with *je vais*).

(duh lotre ko-tay duh)
de l'autre côté de
on the other side (of)

(ah ko-tay duh)
à côté de
next to

(ahN fahs duh)
en face de
facing

(ah gohsh)
à gauche
to the left

(too drwah)
tout droit
straight ahead

(ah drwaht)
à droite
to the right

(ah-lay)
A L L E R
to go

je vais	*(zhuh veh)*	*I go*
tu vas	*(tew vah)*	*you go*
il, elle, on va	*(eel, ehl, ohN vah)*	*he, she one goes*
nous allons	*(noo zah-lohN)*	*we go*
vous allez	*(voo zah-lay)*	*you go*
ils, elles vont	*(eel, ehl vohN)*	*they go*

ORDINAL NUMBERS

You will need to know ordinal numbers when someone gives you directions (telling you which *rue* to turn on). These numbers also come in handy when you need to tell which *étage* (floor) your *chambre d'hôtel* (hotel room) is on, or which *étage* you want to stop on in a *grand magasin* (department store).

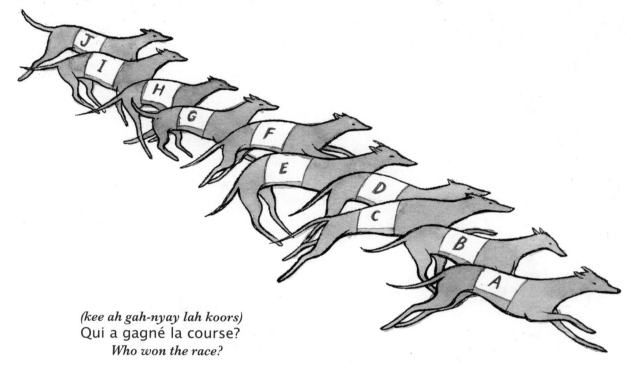

(kee ah gah-nyay lah koors)
Qui a gagné la course?
Who won the race?

Using the numbers on the right, fill in the blanks to help the race announcer announce the winning *chien* (*syaN* = dog) and the first nine runner–ups. Say each number as you write it. Notice the differences in spelling in *cinquième and neuvième*.

A is _____   F is _____

(nuh-vyem)
neuvième

(seh-tyem)
septième

B is _____   G is _____

(kah-tree-yem)
quatrième

(wee-tyem)
huitième

C is _____   H is _____

(pruh-myay)
premier (première)

(dee-zyem)
dixième

D is _____   I is _____

(see-zyem)
sixième

(duh-zyem)
deuxième

E is _____   J is _____

(saN-kyem)
cinquième

(trwah-zyem)
troisième

DIALOG

(mee-shehl ay nee-kohl)   *(uhN no-tehl)*
Michel et Nicole are standing outside *un hôtel* talking.

       (oo vah tew oh-zhoor-dwee)
Michel: Où vas–tu aujourd'hui?
          go

       (zhuh veh o see-nay-mah)
Nicole: Je vais au cinéma.
         to the

       (Meh)   *(seh laN-dee)*   *(eh fehr-may)*
Michel: Mais aujourd'hui c'est lundi. Le cinéma est fermé.
       but   *closed*

       (wee   seh vreh)   *(tahN-pee eh twah)*
Nicole: Oui, c'est vrai. Tant pis! Et toi, où vas–tu?
       that's right   too bad   and you

Michel: *(dah-bohr)* D'abord je vais à la banque. *(ah lah bahNk ahN-sweet)* Ensuite, je vais faire *(fehr day koors)* des courses dans un grand *(dahN zuhN grahN)*
first   *then*   *to go shopping*   *in*   *department*

(mah-gah-zaN) magasin. *(vuh)* Veux–tu *(vuh-neer)* venir avec moi?
store   *to come*

Nicole: Non, merci. *(zhuh pahNs kuh zhehm-ray ah-lay vee-zee-tay uhN mew-zay dahr)* Je pense que j'aimerais aller visiter un musée d'art.
that I would like to go

Michel: Tu *(puh)* peux aller au Musée *(dohr-say)* d'Orsay aujourd'hui. Il est *(eel eh-too-vehr)* ouvert le lundi.
can   *it*   *open*

Nicole: *(zhay-nyahl oo-weh)* Génial! Où est le Musée d'Orsay? C'est *(seh lwaN)* loin?
great

Michel: Non, ce *(seh neh pah)* n'est pas loin... Va *(vah too drwah)* tout droit et *(prahN)* prend la *(preh-myehr rew ah gohsh)* première rue à gauche.
it is not   *go*

(seh) C'est la rue de *(raN-bo)* Rimbaud. *(kohN-tee-new zhew-sko boo-lvahr ah-nah-tohl frahNs)* Continue jusqu'au boulevard Anatole France.
until

(toorn ah drwaht) Ensuite, tourne à droite. Continue jusqu'au *(pohN day zah-moo-ruh)* pont des Amoureux.
bridge of the lovers

(trah-vehrs) Traverse le pont et tourne *(ee-may-dee-aht-mahN)* immédiatement à gauche.
cross

(tew veh-rah) Tu verras le musée *(sewr tah)* sur ta droite.
will see   *on your*

Nicole: *(dah-kohr)* D'accord. Merci, Michel. A *(ah byaN-to)* bientôt!
see you later

Michel: A bientôt! Bonne promenade!
have a good walk

PRACTICE

Comprenez–vous?
Do you understand?

Répondez "oui" ou "non".

1. Est–ce que le cinéma est fermé le mercredi? _____
2. Est–ce que le Musée d'Orsay est ouvert le lundi? _____
3. Est–ce que Nicole veut faire des courses aujourd'hui? _____
4. Est–ce loin d'aller au Musée d'Orsay? _____

CHAPTER 7

(kehl eh tah say-zohN pray-fay-ray)
Quelle est ta saison préférée?
Which season do you prefer?

(ahN dotr moh)
en d'autres mots
in other words

(mwah-o-see)
moi aussi
me too

(ah mohN nah-vee)
à mon avis
in my opinion

(too luh mohNd)
tout le monde
everyone

(duh tahN zahN tahN)
de temps en temps
from time to time

LES SAISONS DE L'ANNÉE

(lay seh-zohN duh lah-nay)
the seasons of the year

Notice that *le printemps* (spring) is different from the other seasons when you want to express "in" before the season.

(zhuh veh ah moN-ray-all ahN-nay-tay)
Je vais à Montréal en été.
I'm going to Montreal in the summer.

(zhuh veh zahN behl-zhee kahN-nee-vehr)
Je vais en Belgique en hiver.
I'm going to Belgium in the winter.

(zhun veh ah la mar-tee-nee kahN-no-tohn)
Je vais à la Martinique en automne.
I'm going to Martinique in autumn (the fall).

(zhuh veh ah nee soh praN-tahN)
Je vais à Nice au printemps.
I'm going to Nice in the spring.

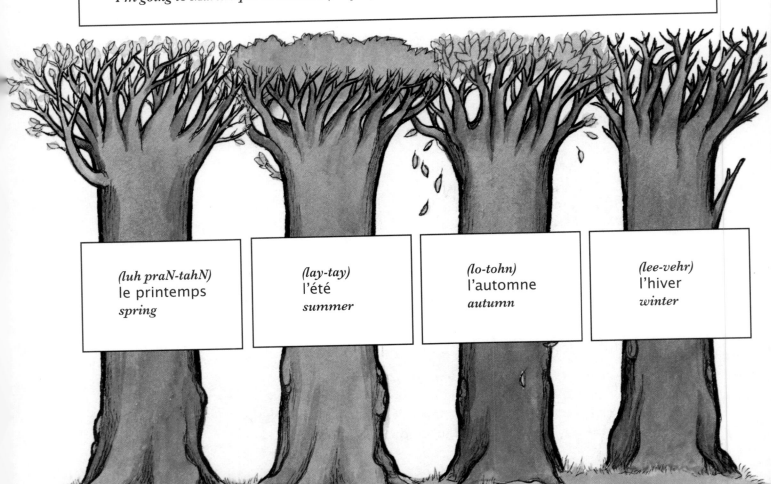

(luh praN-tahN)
le printemps
spring

(lay-tay)
l'été
summer

(lo-tohn)
l'automne
autumn

(lee-vehr)
l'hiver
winter

LES MOIS DE L'ANNÉE

(lay mwah duh lah-nay)
the months of the year

Say each month out loud in French, using the pronunciation key. Try not to read them as you would in English. Remember not to say the "n's" or "m's" as we do in English. The capital *N* means "Put it in your nose." You should feel a slight vibration through your nose when you say a nasal vowel. Drop your jaw (which opens your mouth) when you see *ahN*, and don't close it until you get to the next sound: *day-sahN* (mouth open) *br* (mouth closed) for *décembre*. Notice that the months are not capitalized in French.

(zhahN-vyay)
janvier

(fay-vree-ay)
février

(mahrs)
mars

(ah-vreel)
avril

(meh)
mai

(zhwaN)
juin

(zhwee-yeh)
juillet

(oot)
août

(sehp-tahNbr)
septembre

(ok-tohbr)
octobre

(noh-vahNbr)
novembre

(day-sahNbr)
décembre

STORY

Look at the pictures and read the sentences under each one. See if you can figure out *le sens* (*luh sahNs* = the meaning). Write what you think the sentences mean in the blanks. Use the vocabulary and idioms on the previous pages to help you *comprendre* (*kohN-prahNdr* = to understand) the story that follows the pictures.

(lah mehr)
la mère
mother

(luh pehr)
le père
father

(lah suhr)
la soeur
sister

(luh frehr)
le frère
brother

(lah mehr eh tah lah plazh ahN nay-tay)
La mère est à la plage en été.

1. _____

(luh pehr eh dahN lay mohN-tah nyahN nee-vehr)
Le père est dans les montagnes en hiver.

2. _____

(luh frehr rahN-dohn nahN noh-tohn)
Le frère randonne en automne.

3. _____

(lay suhr ruh-gard lay fluhr oh prahN-tahN)
Les soeurs regardent les fleurs au printemps.

4. _____

(zhuh mah-pehl ee-rehn shah-boh   zhay vaN tahN   zhay ewn fah-mee-y   treh zaN-tay-reh-sahNt)
Je m'appelle Irène Chabot. J'ai 20 ans. J'ai une famille très intéressante. Nous

(sohm) (toos)   *(kahN noo pruh-nohN   day va-kahNs) (mah)*   *(vuh too-zhoor)*
sommes tous différents. Quand nous prenons des vacances, ma mère veut toujours
   are   all   *when*   *wants   always*

(ah-lay ah lah plazh)   *(lay mohN-tah-nyuh)*
aller à la plage, mais mon père aime les montagnes. En d'autres mots, ma mère aime

              (ahN nay-tay sewr-too ahN oot) (mohN)   *(lee-vehr) (ee lehm skee-yay)*
prendre des vacances en été, surtout en août. Mon père préfère l'hiver. Il aime skier
                          especially

                                                (ehm rahN-duh-nay)
en décembre ou en janvier. Mon frère, Robert, qui a 17 ans, aime randonner en
                                                                            to hike
(fo-reh)   *(koo-luhr)*   *(lo-tohm)*   *(dohNk)*
forêt. Il aime les couleurs de l'automne (orange, rouge, jaune, marron). Donc, il
                                                                                      so
(vuh prahNdr)   *(ahN)*   *(oo)*   *(puh-teet)*
veut prendre des vacances en septembre ou octobre. Ma petite soeur Janine, 15
                                                        or
(ahN)
ans, aime le printemps. Moi aussi! Janine et moi aimons les belles fleurs.
                                      (ehmohN) (lay) (behl fluhr)

(cuh-pahN-dahN)   *(nehm pah)*   *(sohN)*
Cependant, ma soeur n'aime pas voyager. A mon avis, mars, avril et mai sont les
however

(plew bo)   *(poor)*   *(kahN   pruh-nohN noo noh)*   *(too-to lohN)*
plus beaux mois pour voyager. Quand prenons–nous nos vacances? Tout au long de
most beautiful   for   *our*

(lah-nay)   *(noo rahN-doh-nohN)*
l'année! Nous randonnons chaque samedi en septembre. De temps en temps, nous

            (o-see ahN nee-vehr)   *(byaN sewr)   (skee-yohN   wee-kehnd)*
randonnons aussi en hiver et au printemps. Bien sûr, nous skions les week–ends en
                                                          of course

                              (oot   noo zah-lohn soo-vahN)
décembre, janvier et février. En juin, juillet et août, nous allons souvent à la plage.
                                                                            often
(reh-stohN oh-see)   *(may-zohN) (aN-see too-luh-mohNd)*
Nous restons aussi souvent à la maison. Ainsi, tout le monde est content.
   stay   also   *at home*   *thus everybody*

PRACTICE

A. See if you can translate the following sentences into *anglais*.

   1. Mon père préfère l'hiver. _____

   2. Mon frère, Robert, qui a 17 ans, aime randonner en forêt.

   _____

   3. Quand prenons-nous nos vacances?
      when

   _____

   4. De temps en temps, nous randonnons aussi en hiver et au printemps.

   _____

B. Now try to translate these sentences into *français*.

   1. I'm 20 years old. _____

   2. He likes the colors of autumn (orange, red, yellow, brown).

   _____

   3. Me too! Janine and I love the beautiful flowers.

   _____

   4. In June, July, and August we often go to the beach.

   _____

FOCUS

All French nouns are either masculine or feminine in gender. Sometimes it's easy to figure out which group a noun belongs to as in *un américain,* an American man, and *une américaine,* an American woman. Other times it just doesn't make any sense: *la cravate* (a necktie) is feminine and *le maquillage* (make-up) is masculine.

Try to learn the noun markers (*le, la, un,* or *une*) together with the nouns: *la plage, la fleur, le printemps, le mois, une famille, un jour.* This will help you a lot in remembering the gender.

FEMININE
la mère

MASCULINE
le père

There are 4 different ways of
saying "the" (the definite article):

le, la, l', les

l'automne (masculine, but also is used with feminine
nouns that begin with a vowel as in *l'amie* – or an *h* as in *l'heure*)

les vacances (plural – masculine and feminine)

Choose the definite article that goes with each noun.
You may have to look back at previous chapters!

1. _____ soeur

2. _____ plage

3. _____ famille

4. _____ fromage

5. _____ voiture

6. _____ homme

7. _____ matin

8. _____ saison

9. _____ musée

10. _____ rue

There are 2 different ways of saying "a" (the indefinite article):

un mois (masculine), *une maison* (feminine).

Unlike English, French also has a plural form of the indefinite article, *des* (some):

des montagnes, des fleurs

CHAPTER 8

(vwah-see mah fah-mee-y)
Voici ma famille.
This is my family.

There is a good chance that if you make *un ami français* or *une amie française* you will be introduced to some of his or her family members at some point. Not only is it important to be able to understand these words that show family relationships, but it's also useful to be able to introduce and talk about the members of your family.

(luh shah-po)
le chapeau
hat

(day lew-neht)
des lunettes
glasses

(grahN/grahNd)
grand/grande
tall

(lay shuh-vuh)
les cheveux
hair

(lohN/lohNg)
long/longue
long

(puh-tee/puh-teet)
petit/petite
short

(luh mah-ree)
le mari
husband

(lah fahm)
la femme
wife

FOCUS: FAMILY

MALE

le père	*(luh pehr)*	*father*
le grand–père	*(luh grahN-pehr)*	*grandfather*
le beau–père	*(luh bo-pehr)*	*father-in-law*
le frère	*(luh frehr)*	*brother*
le beau–frère	*(luh bo-frehr)*	*brother-in law*
le fils	*(luh fees)*	*son*
le petit–fils	*(luh puh-tee-fees)*	*grandson*
l'oncle	*(lohNkl)*	*uncle*
le neveu	*(luh nuh-vuh)*	*nephew*
le mari	*(luh mah-ree)*	*husband*

FEMALE

la mère	*(lah mehr)*	*mother*
la grand–mère	*(lah grahN- mehr)*	*grandmother*
la belle–mère	*(lah behl-mehr)*	*mother-in-law*
la soeur	*(lah suhr)*	*sister*
la belle–soeur	*(lah behl-suhr)*	*sister-in-law*
la fille	*(lah fee-y)*	*daughter*
		("la fille" also means "girl")
la petite–fille	*(lah puh-teet fee-y)*	*granddaughter*
la tante	*(lah tahNt)*	*aunt*
la nièce	*(lah nyehs)*	*niece*
la femme	*(lah fahm)*	*wife*

STORY

(pee-yeh-rah ewn puh-teet fa-mee-y sa mehr sah-pehl soh-fee)   (ehl ah day shuh-vuh koor)
Pierre a une petite famille. Sa mère s'appelle Sophie. Elle a des cheveux courts, gris
    has

(eh)   (dee-nah-meek) (sohN pehr)   (ruh-nay) (eel eh grahN)
et elle est très dynamique. Son père s'appelle René. Il est grand
    is

(ay ehm) (pohr-tay uhN shah-po)   (nah pah duh suhr meh)   (frehr)
et aime porter un chapeau. Pierre n'a pas de soeurs mais il a un frère,
    wear   *doesn't have any*

(pah-treek kee lehm bo-koo)   (mah-rahN)   (mah-ree-yay) (mohr-gahn)
Patrick, qu'il aime beaucoup. Patrick est très marrant. Il est marié avec Morgane,
    loves   *funny*

  (behl-suhr)   (ah duh lohN shuh-vuh nwahr)
la belle-soeur de Pierre. Elle a de longs cheveux noirs et elle est belle et très sympa.
                                                       beautiful   *nice*

(eel nohN pas dahN-fahN)   (sah-pehl ay-lehn) (sohN mah-ree)
Ils n'ont pas d'enfants. La belle-mère de Pierre s'appelle Hélène et son mari s'appelle
 don't have any

(ahl-behr)   (bo-pehr)   (lah fahm)   (ahN-dray) (ah day)
Albert. Il est le beau-père de Pierre. La femme de Pierre s'appelle Andrée. Elle a des
                                        wife

      (braN)   (eh puh-tee tay treh zaN-teh-lee-zhahNt eel zohN tuhN nahN-fahN) (ah-play)
cheveux bruns, est petite et très intelligente. Ils ont un enfant, une fille appelée
                                                 they have   *girl*

(nah-tah-lee)   (ohN zahN)   (sah)   (sewr-too say grahN-pah-rahN)
Nathalie. Elle a 11 ans et adore sa famille, surtout ses grands-parents.   Nathalie

(pohrt day lew-neht)   (bo meh pah treh zaN-teh-lee-gahN)
porte des lunettes. Et Pierre? Il est beau mais pas très intelligent.
wears   *handsome*   *not*

PRACTICE

Fill in the blanks under each picture.
   a) Write the name of the person.
   b) Write what relationship that person is to Pierre. (Be sure to include the definite article *le, la,* or *les* before the word.)

(Pierre)

1. a _____
   b _____
2. a _____
   b _____

3. a _____
   b _____
4. a _____
   b _____

5. a _____
   b _____

6. a _____
   b _____
7. a _____
   b _____

8. a _____
   b _____

Now see if you can answer these questions. Check your answers in the back of the book.

1. *(kee)*
   Qui est très intelligente? _____

2. *who*
   Qui a les cheveux courts et gris? _____

3. Qui est marié avec Morgane? _____

4. Qui aime ses grand-parents? _____

5. Qui est beau? _____

FOCUS : ADJECTIVES

In English, adjectives don't change according to the nouns they describe: the tall girl, the tall boy, the tall women – "tall" stays the same. In French, however, the adjective must agree with the noun in gender (masculine or feminine) and number (singular or plural): *la grande fille, le grand garçon, les grandes femmes.*

To make masculine adjectives feminine, you usually had an "e": *court/courte, grand/grande, intelligent/intelligente.* Add "s" to the masculine or feminine form to make the plural *(les grandes femmes).* Short, common adjectives are placed in front of the noun *(petite famille),* but in general, adjectives are placed after the nouns they describe: *une femme intelligente.* This holds true for colors too (chapter 5): *la lune bleue* (the blue moon), *la maison blanche* (the white house – *"blanche"* is an irregular feminine form of *"blanc"*), *les lunettes noires* (the black glasses).

Add the French form of the adjective to each of the nouns:

1. la femme (tall)   la grande femme _____

2. la fille (short)   _____

3. le mari (handsome)   _____

4. la grand-mère (beautiful) _____

5. la nièce (intelligent) _____

6. les pères (intelligent) _____

POSSESSIVE ADJECTIVES

Words like: "my", "your", "his", "her" are possessive adjectives. Just as the definite articles *(le, la, les)* have to agree with the noun, so do the possessive adjectives. Look at the chart on the next page. Notice that in contrast to English, the possessive adjectives in French agree with the thing possessed, not the person who possesses.

A word on pronunciation: in the masculine form with *oncle* you must make the link in pronunciation because *oncle* begins with a vowel: *mon oncle = mohN-nohNkl.* (The "n" sound links to *oncle* so it sounds like one word.)

FEMININE			MASCULINE	
With feminine nouns			*With masculine nouns*	
ma tante	(mah tahNt)	MY	mon oncle	(mohN-nohNkl)
mes tantes	(may tahNt)		mes oncles	(may-zohNkl)
ta tante	(tah tahNt)	YOUR (familiar)	ton oncle	(tohN-nohNkl)
tes tantes	(tay tahNt)		tes oncles	(tay-zohNkl)
votre tante	(vohtr tahNt)	YOUR (plural & polite)	votre oncle	(vo-trohNkl)
vos tantes	(vo tahNt)		vos oncles	(vo-zohNkl)
sa tante	(sah tahNt)	HIS/HER	son oncle	(sohN-nohNkl)
ses tantes	(say tahNt)		ses oncles	(say-zohNkl)
notre tante	(nohtr tahNt)	OUR	notre oncle	(no-trohNkl)
nos tantes	(no tahNt)		nos oncles	(no-zohNkl)
leur tante	(luhr tahNt)	THEIR	leur oncle	(luh-rohNkl)
leurs tantes	(luhr tahNt)		leurs oncles	(luhr zohNkl)

PRACTICE

Now see if you can put the appropriate possessive adjective in front of the following nouns:

1. _____ famille
   my

2. _____ maison
   his

3. _____ père
   her

4. _____ soeur
   your (familiar)

5. _____ frères
   their

6. _____ chapeau
   your (polite)

7. _____ amis
   my

8. _____ mère
   their

9. _____ femme
   his

10. _____ parents
   our

CHAPTER 9

(kehl tahN feh-teel)
Quel temps fait–il?
What's the weather?

Being able to chat about *le temps (luh tahN - the weather)* is a useful skill to have in another language. Whether you're at a bus stop, *au restaurant (oh res-toh-rahN),* or making small talk with a desk clerk at a hotel, *le temps* is a safe, popular, topic (and often necessary if you're planning outdoor activities).

A few things to remember: The French do not say "It IS cold" (like we do in English). They use *faire* when they talk about the weather: *Il fait froid.* ("It MAKES cold.") The *il* in weather phrases does not mean "he", nor does it refer to a masculine object. It means "it" as in "It's raining." Notice that *Il pleut* and *Il neige* do not use *faire.*

When you want to say "I AM cold" or "I AM hot" do NOT translate those expressions directly into French (using "am"). Your meaning may be misinterpreted. Instead, say "I HAVE cold" *(J'ai froid – zhay frwah)* or "I HAVE hot" *(J'ai chaud – zhay sho).*

N O T E : You may remember from Chapter 2: *J'ai faim* (I am hungry.) Go back to Chapter 3 to review the different forms of *avoir* (to have) and to see other expressions using *avoir.*

(eel feh sho)
Il fait chaud.
It's hot.

(eel feh frwah)
Il fait froid.
It's cold.

(eel feh dew vahN)
Il fait du vent.
It's windy.

(eel pluh)
Il pleut.
It's raining.

(eel feh dew soh-lay)
Il fait du soleil.
It's sunny.

(eel feh bo)
Il fait beau.
It's beautiful.

(eel feh moh-veh)
Il fait mauvais.
It's horrible.

(eel nehzh)
Il neige.
It's snowing.

DIALOG

This is a telephone conversation between *Elise et sa mère*. *Elise a 22 ans* and is living in Alaska for 1 year doing research as part of her university graduate studies. *Sa mère* lives in *Paris*.

(bohN-zhoor mah-mahN)
Elise: Bonjour, maman.

(mah shay-ree kohN-mahN vah tew)
Maman: Bonjour, ma chérie. Comment vas–tu?

(zhuh veh byaN sohf kuh zhay frwah)
Elise: Je vais bien sauf que j'ai froid.
  I'm well   except

(mah pohvr puh-teet   eel nehzh)
Maman: Ma pauvre petite…. Il neige?

(seh lee-vehr)   (swee zahN)
Elise: Maman, c'est l'hiver et je suis en Alaska.

(ee-lee-ya)   (ee-see)
Bien sûr, il y a beaucoup de neige ici.
  there is   here

(kehl tahN feh-teel ah pah-ree)
Quel temps fait–il à Paris?

(eel pluh)   (o-zhoor-dwee)
Maman: Il pleut beaucoup aujourd'hui.

(yehr ee-lee-yah-veh dew soh-lehy)
Mais hier, il y avait du soleil. En fait, il
  yesterday, there was   in fact

(fuh-zeh)   (eel feh frwa)
faisait très chaud hier mais il fait froid
it was

(ee-lee-o-rah)   (duh-maN)
aujourd'hui. Il y aura du soleil demain.
          there will be sun   tomorrow

(kahN ruh-vyaN-tew)
Quand reviens–tu à la maison?

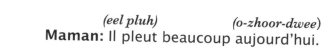

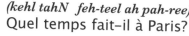
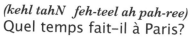

Elise: *(zhuh nseh pah)* Je ne sais pas. *(byaN oh-kew-pay pahr may ruh-shehrsh)* Je suis bien occupée par mes recherches.
I don't know

(zhuh trah-vahy   too lay zhoor sof)
Je travaille tous les jours sauf le dimanche.
work   everyday   except

Maman: Oh mon Dieu! Où travailles–tu?
oh my goodness

Elise: *(prahN lah-vyohN poor)* Je prends l'avion pour Nome tous les
every

(luhN-dee ay zhee rehstsoo-vahN)
lundi et j'y reste souvent deux jours. Je vais souvent
I stay there   often

(ahN vwa-tewr)   (o-see) (seh lwaN dee-see)
en voiture à Fairbanks aussi. C'est loin d'ici!
from here

(pray-fehr)
Je préfère travailler à Anchorage.

(dwah ruh-toor-nay)   (suh)   (kahN vyaN)   (muh rahNdr vee-zeet)
Je dois retourner à Fairbanks ce vendredi. Quand viens–tu me rendre visite?
this   me   to visit

Maman: Oh mon Dieu, pas maintenant! Pas pendant l'hiver! Tu sais que je n'aime pas
not   during   know that

(vuh vuh-nee-rahN nay-tay)   (fuh-rah sho)
la neige. Je veux venir en été, quand il fera chaud.
it will be

Elise: D'accord. Oui, il fait trop froid ici en hiver.

Je reviendrai peut–être pour les vacances.
will go back perhaps

(kehl boh nee-day)   (ruh-vyaN)
Maman: Quelle bonne idée! Reviens à la maison, chérie.
what a   come back

(kohm)   (luh seh)   (duh tahN zahN tahN)
Comme tu le sais, il y a du soleil de temps en temps ici.
as   from time to time

Et pas de neige!

Elise: OK, maman. A bientôt.

Maman: Au revoir, ma chérie. Bon courage!
keep your chin up

PRACTICE

Comprenez-vous?
Do you understand?

See if you can answer the following questions based on the dialog.

(kee)
1. Qui a froid? _____
   who

2. Où est Elise? _____

3. Où pleut-il? _____

4. Quand Elise travaille-t-elle? _____

See if you can match the numbers of each statement on the right to the appropriate picture of the person to make each statement true. The first one is done for you.

① Elle dit qu'il pleut.

② Elle a froid.

③ Elle travaille du lundi au samedi.

④ Elle dit qu'elle n'aime pas la neige.

⑤ Elle va travailler en avion et en voiture.

⑥ Elle veut aller en Alaska en été.

⑦ Elle reviendra à la maison en avion en décembre.

⑧ Elle aime travailler à Anchorage.

PRACTICE

Quel temps fait–il?
What's the weather?

Let's see if you can complete the sentences with the weather expressions given. (You can peak back at Chapter 7 to review *les mois et les saisons*.)

1. En été _____.
   it is hot

2. En avril _____.
   it rains a lot

3. En novembre _____.
   it's bad weather

4. En janvier _____.
   it snows

5. Au printemps _____.
   it is windy

6. En juillet _____.
   it's humid

7. Aujourd'hui _____.
   it's beautiful

EXPRESSIONS FOR TIME

You may recall the words *hier* (yesterday) and *aujourd'hui* (today) from Chapter 6 when you learned about giving directions. Now let's add *demain* (tomorrow) to your vocabulary. (Remember how *maman* described *le temps à Paris?*)

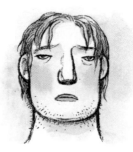

(yehr)
hier
yesterday

(oh-zhoor-dwee)
aujourd'hui
today

(duh-maN)
demain
tomorrow

Here are some useful time expressions:

(lah suh-mehn dehr-nyehr)
la semaine dernière
last week

(ah-vahN tyehr)
avant–hier
the day before yesterday

(lah suh-mehn proh-shehn)
la semaine prochaine
next week

(ah-preh duh-maN)
après demain
the day after tomorrow

PRACTICE AND REVIEW

See if you can figure out which word doesn't belong in each of the series of words below. Write the words in the blanks.

_____ 1. chaud, été, soleil, neige

_____ 2. hier, froid, demain, aujourd'hui

_____ 3. beaucoup, quand, où, qui

_____ 4. travaille, visite, ici, va

_____ 5. jour, semaine, année, printemps

(fehr)
FAIRE
to make/do

je fais	*(zhuh feh)*	*I make, do*
tu fais	*(tew feh)*	*you make, do*
il, elle, on fait	*(eel, ehl, ohN feh)*	*he, she, one makes*
nous faisons	*(noo fuh-zohN)*	*we make, do*
vous faites	*(voo feht)*	*you make, do*
ils, elles font	*(eel, ehl fohN)*	*they make, do*

CHAPTER 10

(voo-za-vay luhr, seel-voo-pleh)
Vous avez l'heure, s'il vous plaît?
Do you have the time, please?

You've learned *les jours de la semaine* (Chapter 5) *et les mois de l'année* (Chapter 7). Now it's time to learn about how to tell time. If you need to, go back to Chapters 2 and 4 to review *les nombres* up to 22. Later in this chapter you'll learn some more numbers that you'll need in order to say the minutes.

(ehtr duh boh new-muhr)
être de bonne humeur
to be in a good mood

(ehtr duh moh-veh-zew-muhr)
être de mauvaise humeur
to be in a bad mood

(eh-trahN nah-vahNs)
être en avance
to be early

(eh-trahN ruh-tahr)
être en retard
to be late

(lah gahr)
la gare
railroad station

(luh bee-yeh/leh bee-yeh)
le billet/les billets
ticket/tickets

(luh keh)
le quai
track

(lah gahr)
la gare
railroad station

(ewn mee-newt/deh mee-newt)
une minute/des minutes
minute/minutes

(zewt)
Zut!
Darn!

DIALOG

Antoine et Florence arrivent à la gare. Ils veulent prendre le train pour rendre visite à
(luhr zah-mee nees)
leurs amis à Nice.
their

(seel voo pleh)   (poo-vay-voo meh)   (deer kahN pahr luh)
Antoine: S'il vous plaît, pouvez–vous me dire quand part le

(proh-shaN traN poo-uhr nees)
prochain train pour Nice?

Employé: Il part à 10:19.

(ko-mahN)   (ah keh luhr)
Antoine: Comment? A quelle heure?
at what

(muh-syuh)
Employé: 10:19, monsieur.

(eh-teel mahN-tnahN)
Antoine: Quelle heure est–il maintenant?
now

(voo zah-vey)   (mee-newt)
Employé: Il est 10:16. Vous avez trois minutes.
have

(dee)   (ee-lee-ya)   (dahN)
Antoine dit à Florence: Il y a un train dans trois minutes!
says   *there is*

(zewt pah duh shahNs ohN neh tahN ruh-tahr)
Florence: Zut! Pas de chance. On est en retard.
no luck   we

(seh too-zhoor)   (meh mee-stahwr)
Antoine: C'est toujours la même histoire.
always   same story

(noo sohm)   (ahN ruh tahr)
Nous sommes toujours en retard.
we   are

Florence: Tu es de mauvaise humeur
aujourd'hui, non?

(sa sew-fee)
Antonio: Ça suffit!
that's enough

Florence *(à l'employé)* :
(ah lahN-plwah-yay)
A quelle heure part le prochain train pour Nice? Nous ne
(pahr luh proh-shaN traN poor nees)

pouvons pas attraper ce train.
(poo-vohN pah zah-trah-pay seh)
can't catch   this

Employé: Voyons......le prochain train pour Nice part à 13:47.
(vwah-yohN)   *(pahr)*
let's see   leaves

Florence regarde Antoine.
(ruh-gahrd)

Antoine: C'est cool.
(seh kool)

Florence *(à l'employé):* Ça marche.
(sah mahrsh)
that works

Deux billets, s'il vous plaît.
(duh bee-yeh)

Employé: Aller simple ou aller–retour?
(ah-lay saNpl oo ah-lay ruh-toor)
one-way   round-trip

Florence: Aller–retour, s'il vous plaît.

En deuxième classe.
(ahN duh-zyem klahs)

Employé: Ça fait 30 euros. Voici vos billets...
(sah feh)   *(vwah-see voh)*
that makes   here are your

Florence: Merci. quel quai?
(kehl keh)
which

Employee: Le quai numéro 8. Bon voyage!
(new-may-ro) *(bohn vwah-yazh)*
have a good trip

(ah-lohN-zee)
Allons–y!
Let's go!

Antoine *(à Florence)* : Bien...alors, veux-tu prendre un verre?...
(byaN ah-lohr vuh tew prahN druhN vehr)
good   then   to have a drink

Florence: Avec plaisir! C'est étonnant. Tu es de bonne humeur maintenant!
(ah-vehk pleh-zeer seh ay-tohn-nahN)   *(eh duh boh new-muhr maN-tnahN)*
pleasure   amazing

Antoine: Bien sûr. Nous ne sommes plus en retard maintenant. Nous sommes en avance!
(noo nuh sohm plew zahN)   *(sohm zahN ah-vahNs)*
no longer

DO YOU UNDERSTAND?

Answer True or False to the following statements based on the dialog.

_____ 1. Antoine et Florence voyagent en avion.

plane

(duh-mahNd)

_____ 2. Antoine demande l'heure.

asks

(pahNs kuh)

_____ 3. Antoine pense que Florence est de mauvaise humeur.

thinks that

_____ 4. Florence demande trois billets.

_____ 5. Ils vont faire l'aller–retour.

to do

WHAT TIME IS IT?

(keh luh reh teel)
Quelle heure est–il?
What time is it? (This is another way to ask the time.)

Expressing time in French is simple. Just say the number of the hour followed by the word *heure(s)*. If it's not clear from the context, you need to state whether the time is *du matin* (AM), *de l'après-midi* (PM) for the afternoon, or *du soir* (PM) for the evening.

In Europe as well as in French-speaking Canada, the 24-hour system of telling time ("military" time as we call it in the U.S.) is usually used on TV and radio, with travel schedules, appointments, and theater and concert times in order to avoid ambiguity. Just subtract 12 to figure out the time you are familiar with in the U.S. (16 hours is 16–12= 4 PM)

(eel eh seh tuhr)
Il est sept heures
du matin.

Il est midi.

(trwah-zuhr)
Il est trois heures
de l'après–midi.

(wee-tuhr)
Il est huit heures
du soir.

(dew mah-taN)
du matin
in the morning

(mee-dee)
midi
noon

(duh lah-preh-mee-dee)
de l'après-midi
in the afternoon

(dew swahr)
du soir
in the evening

Here are the ways to add the minutes when you are telling time:

(ohN zuhr)
Il est onze heures

(kah-rahNt)
quarante du matin.

(seh tuhr)
Il est sept heures

(vaN)
vingt du matin.

(trwah zuhr)
Il est trois heures

(mwaN dees)
moins dix de l'après-midi.
minus

(nuh vuhr)
Il est neuf heures

(ay duh-mee)
et demie du matin.
half

Note: *heures* is abbreviated to *h* when the time is written in numbers: 7h15 (or 19h15 using the 24–hour clock).

Other possibilities to say the time:

1. You can also say the time and add the minutes instead of saying the next hour
    moins (minus) the minutes: 2:50 is also: *(duh zuhr)*   *(sahN-kahNt)*
                                                          Il est deux heures cinquante.

2. For 8:15, you can use *et quart* (and a quarter) or use the number of minutes: *Il est huit heures quinze.*

3. For 8:45, you could say either:
    Il est huit heures quarante-cinq or *Il est neuf heures moins le quart.*
    (Notice with *moins* it is <u>*le quart,*</u> not <u>*et quart.*</u>)

4. For 9:30, you can use *et demie* (half) or use the number of minutes:
    Il est neuf heures trente.

Match the times with the clocks. Write the correct letter under each clock.

a. Il est dix heures et quart.   b. Il est trois heures quarante–cinq.
c. Il est onze heures trente–huit.   d. Il est cinq heures et demie.
e. Il est huit heures cinquante.

1. _____   2. _____   3. _____   4. _____   5. _____

NUMBERS 23-100

You'll need to know higher *nombres* if you want to understand *les minutes* when someone tells you the time (...not to mention how important these numbers are for shopping or even revealing your age if the situation presents itself.) Read the pronunciation carefully and say each number out loud.

There are three things you should notice about these higher numbers that will help you memorize them.

1. Use *et* (and) only in the numbers 21, 31, 41, 51, 61, and 71. Use a hyphen in all others up to 99.

2. Don't use the word *un* (one) in 100 *(cent)* *(sahN)* or in 1000 *(mille)* *(meel)*.

3. The numbers from 70 to 100 involve doing some math. Look at these examples:

70 = 60+10   81 = 4 x 20 + 1
75 = 60+15   89 = 4 x 20 + 9
80 = 4 x 20   90 = 80 + 10

In Switzerland and Belgium, however, the old forms of *septante (sehp-tahNt)* (70), sometimes *huitante (ew-ee-tahNt)* (80), and *nonante (nohnaNt)* (90) are used - and are easier to remember!

23	vingt–trois	*(vaN- trwah)*	40	quarante	*(kah-rahNt)*
24	vingt–quatre	*(vaN-kahtr)*	50	cinquante	*(saN-kahNt)*
25	vingt–cinq	*(vaN-saNk)*	60	soixante	*(swah-sahNt)*
26	vingt–six	*(vaN-sees)*	70	soixante–dix	*(swah-sahNt-dees)*
27	vingt–sept	*(vaN-seht)*	71	soixante et onze	*(swah-sahN-tay-ohNz)*
28	vingt–huit	*(vaN-weet)*	72	soixante–douze	*(swah-sahNt-dooz)*
29	vingt–neuf	*(vaN-nuhf)*	80	quatre–vingts	*(kahtr-vaN)*
30	trente	*(trahNt)*	85	quatre–vingt–cinq	*(kahtr-vaN-sahNk)*
31	trent–et–un	*(trahN-tay-uhN)*	90	quartre–vingt–dix	*(kahtr-vaN-dees)*
32	trente–deux	*(trahNt-duh)*	100	cent	*(sahN)*

CHAPTER 11

(kuh feh-tew pahN-dahN tohN tahN leebr)
Que fais–tu pendant ton temps libre?
What do you do in your free time?

(prohpr koh muhN soo nuhf)
propre comme un sou neuf
neat as a pin

(o puh-tee mah-taN)
au petit matin
at the crack of dawn

(uhN faN kew-ee-zee-nyay)
un fin cuisinier
a real gourmet cook

FOCUS: PREPOSITIONS

(dahN)
dans
in

(duh-vahN)
devant
in front of

(soo)
sous
under

(duh-dahN)
dedans
inside

(sewr)
sur
on

(deh-ryehr)
derrière
behind

(ahN dohr duh)
en dehors de
outside

(ah ko-tay duh)
à côté (de)
next to

USEFUL EXPRESSIONS

(vwah-lah)
voilà
there is/there are

(sewr-fay sewr luh wehb)
surfer sur le Web
surf the Web

(ahN-vwa-yay uhN ee-mehl)
envoyer un email
send email

VOCABULARY

(ahN bah)
en bas
downstairs

(ahN-o)
en haut
upstairs

(luh shyaN)
le chien
dog

(lay pehr-sohn)
les personnes
people

(zhuhn)
jeune
young

(lohr-dee-nah-tuhr)
l'ordinateur (m)
computer

(luh shah/lah shaht)
le chat(m)/la chatte (f)
cat

(vyuh)   *(vyay)*
vieux (m)/vieille (f)
old

STORY

(sah-mee eh-tuhN puh-tee shyaN mah-rohN) (eelah-beet)   *(ah-veh kewn shaht nwahr kee)*
Sami est un petit chien marron.   Il habite dans une maison avec une chatte noire qui
                          live

     (mo-vehz)   *(eelya)*   *(pehr-sohn kee ah-bee to-see)*   *(seht meh-zohN)*
s'appelle Mauvaise. Il y a trois personnes qui habitent aussi dans cette maison: une
                                                           this

(fahm   uhN vyay-ohm)   *(uhN zhun gahr-sohN)*
femme, un vieil homme, et un jeune garçon.

Leur maison est propre comme un
                     (rahN soo-vahN vee-zee ta)
sou neuf. Sami rend souvent visite à

(lewk   ahN-fahN)
Luc, un enfant de sept ans, dans sa chambre

              (ehm sahswahr)   *(lee)*
en haut. Sami aime s'asseoir sur le lit

(pahN-dahN kuh)   *(zhoo)*   *(seh zhoo-ay)*
pendant que Luc joue avec ses jouets.

   (mo-vehz)   *(dohr)*
Mauvaise, la chatte, dort sous le lit.
                sleeps (from dormir)

(to-mah)   *(pah-say dew)*
Thomas, le grand–père de Luc, aime passer du

(tahN dahN kwee-zeen) (ah-dohr kwee-zee-nay)
temps dans la cuisine. Il adore cuisiner.
                 to cook

                             (ah ko-tay dew foor)   *(puh ah-lohr sahN-teer)*
En fait, il est un fin cuisinier. Sami aime s'asseoir à côté du four. Il peut alors sentir de
                                                      can then smell

(day-lee-see-yuh zo-duhr)   *(kwee-zeen)*   *(tah-pee)*   *(fuh-nehtr)*
délicieuses odeurs quand Thomas cuisine. Mauvaise dort sur le tapis devant la fenêtre.
     smells   *rug*   *window*

         (fehr lah grahs mah-tee-nay)   *(kah-treen)*   *(suh lehv)*
Sami aime "faire la grasse matinée", mais Catherine, la mère de Luc, se lève au petit
         to sleep in   *gets up*

     (vah)   *(sohN bew-ro)* *(meh ahN root) (sohN nohr-dee-nah-tuhr) (lee say zee-mehl sewrf)*
matin, va en bas à son bureau et met en route son ordinateur. Elle lit ses emails et surfe
     goes   *office*   *boots up*   *reads*

(dohr) *(kohr-beh yah pah-pyay)*
sur le Web. Mauvaise dort dans la corbeille à papier.
sleeps *wastepaper basket*

(o-see leer)
Catherine aime aussi lire des
to read

(ro-mahN trah-vah-yay) *(zhahr-dahN)*
romans et travailler dans son jardin
novels *work* *garden*

(tahN leebr)
dans son temps libre.
free time

(zhoo-ay dew pee-ah-no) *(suh kahsh)*
Luc aime jouer du piano. Sami se cache
to play piano *hides*

(kah-nah-pay) *(sah-lohN)*
derrière le canapé dans le salon quand Luc
sofa *livingroom*

(nehm pah brew-ee)
joue du piano. Mauvaise n'aime pas le bruit.
noise

(ah-lohr)
Alors, elle va dehors et dort dans le
so

(prehsk too lay vahN-druh-dee) *(vohN)* *(ruh-gahr-day)*
jardin. Presque tous les vendredis, Thomas, Catherine et Luc vont en haut regarder la
almost every Friday *go* *watch*

(tay-lay) *(leevr oo)* *(o kahrt)* *(sahl duh zhuh)*
télé, lire des livres, ou jouer aux cartes dans la salle de jeux. Mauvaise dort sur la
TV *read books* *or* *cards* *game room*

(shehz) *(sah-syay)* *(preh)*
chaise et Sami s'assied par terre près de sa famille.
sits *near*

(ah ewn vee ah-say kohN-fohr-tahbl)
Sami a une vie assez confortable.
life *quite*

DO YOU UNDERSTAND?

(keh skeel-zehm fehr)
Qu'est-ce qu'ils aiment faire? (What do they like to do?) Match the members of the family with the things they like to do. Write the letters in the blanks.

1. Sami aime _____

A. jouer du piano

2. Mauvaise aime _____

B. cuisiner

3. Catherine aime _____

C. dormir

4. Thomas aime _____

D. rendre visite à
la salle de Luc

5. Luc aime _____

E. surfer sur le Web

(eh-may)
AIMER
to like, to love

Aimer is a common French verb that is used for people and things that you like or love. *Adorer* is another verb you can use when you want to say you love or adore someone or something. *Je t'aime (zhuh tehm)* and *Je t'adore (zhuh tah-dohr)* both mean "I love you".

j'aime	*(zhehm)*	*I like, love*
tu aimes	*(tew ehm)*	*you like, love*
il, elle, on aime	*(eel, ehl, ohN ehm)*	*he, she, one likes, loves*
nous aimons	*(noo zehmohN)*	*we like, love*
vous aimez	*(voo zehmay)*	*you like, love*
ils, elles aiment	*(eel, ehl zehm)*	*they like, love*

PRACTICE

Use the picture below to help you fill in the blanks with *dans, sur, sous, à côté de ou derrière*.

1. L'homme est _____ le lit.

2. Il y a une chatte _____ le lit.
   there is

3. Le lit est _____ le tapis.

4. La fenêtre est _____ le lit.

5. Il y a des jouets _____ le lit.

6. Il y a une corbeille à papier _____ du lit.

Now write 2 sentences of your own describing the picture.

1. _____

2. _____

CHAPTER 12

(ah-tew pah-say uhN bohN wee-kend)
As–tu passé un bon week end?
Did you have a good weekend?

(seh luhN-dee mah-tahN vaN-sahN ay mohN-neek sohN to tra-vahy)
C'est lundi matin. Vincent et Monique sont au travail.
                                                    are   at   work

Vincent: Bonjour, Monique. As–tu passé un bon week end?

(say-teh zhay-nyahl)
Monique: Bonjour, Vincent. Oui, c'était génial.
                        it was great

(keh-skuh tew ah feh)
Vincent: Ah bon? Qu'est–ce que tu as fait?
     really   what did you do

(zhay zhoo-ay o teh-nees)
Monique: Samedi j'ai joué au tennis.

(swee zah-lay vwahr uhN kohN-sehr)
Samedi soir je suis allée voir un concert
        I went   to see

(sew-pehr)
des Rolling Stones. C'était super!

(luhr mew-zeek)
Vincent: J'adore leur musique.

(frahNsh-mahN)
Franchement, je suis surpris
frankly

(keel   zhoo ahN-kohr)
qu'ils jouent encore.
that   are still playing

Monique: Qu'est-ce que tu as fait ce week end? As-tu joué au foot comme d'habitude?
(o foot   kohm dah-bee-tewd)
did   you play soccer   as usual

Vincent: Oui, j'ai joué au foot samedi et hier soir j'ai regardé un film avec mon neveu.
(zhay joo-ay)   *(yehr swahr)*   *(feelm)*   *(nuh-vuh)*
I played   *nephew*

Monique: Quel film, avez-vous vu?
(kehl)   *(ah-vay voo vew)*
did you see

Vincent: On a vu le nouveau film de Harry Potter.
(ohN nah vew noo-vo)   *(ah-ree po-tehr)*
new

Monique: Oh! Il est bien?

Vincent: Oui, J'ai pensé que c'était très amusant,
(zhay pahN-say   say-teh treh zah-mew-zahN)

mais mon neveu a eu un peu peur.
(ah ew uhN puh puhr)
was a little afraid

Monique: Ma fille veut le voir, mais moi,
(fee-y)   *(mwah)*
it

je préfère les films romantiques.
(ro-mahN-teek)

Vincent: Oh, vraiment? Moi aussi.
(vreh-mahN mwah-o-see)
really   me too

Monique: Allez, tu blagues!
(blahg)
come on you're joking

Vincent: Non, je ne blague pas!

On se verra à la réunion ce matin.
(ohN suh vehr-rah) (ray-ew-nyohN)
we'll see each other at the meeting

Monique: Zut! Quelle réunion?
(zewt   kehl)
darn   what

MATCHING

Match the questions and statements on the left with the appropriate responses on the right.

_____ 1. Qu'est-ce que tu as fait ce week end?   a) Oui, j'ai passé un bon week end.

_____ 2. As-tu passé un bon week end?   b) Quel film as-tu vu?

_____ 3. J'ai vu un film hier soir.   c) J'ai joué au foot.

_____ 4. Comment était le concert?   d) Oui.
                     how

_____ 5. Tu blagues!   e) C'était génial!

_____ 6. Il est bien?   f) Non! Je ne blague pas.

SIMPLE PAST TENSE VERBS

There are several past tenses in French, as there are in English. The passé composé *(pah-say kohN-po-zay)* is most commonly used as the past tense in French. It is a compound tense, which means it is made up of two parts: a helping verb *avoir (ah-vwahr)* (have) or *être (ehtr)* (be) and a past participle *J'ai <u>vu</u> (zhay vew)* (I saw), *J'ai <u>pensé</u> (zhay pahN-say)* (I thought), *Je suis <u>allé</u> (zhuh swee zah-lay)* (I went).

Most of the time in American English we don't use the helping verb. Instead of "I have eaten" we would say in English "I ate." The helping verb ("have"-*ai*- in this case) must be used in French: *J'ai mangé (zhay mahN-zhay)* ("I ate.").

To form the *passé composé* use the present tense of the helping verb plus a past participle. For verbs that end in -er in infinitive form (like *penser - pahN-say* - to think), just take off the -er from the verb *(pens)* and add -é *(pensé)*.

(pahN-say)

PENSER (passé composé)

to think

J'ai pensé	*(zhay pahN-say)*	*I thought*
Tu as pensé	*(tew ah pahN-say)*	*you thought*
Il, elle, on a pensé	*(eel, ehl, ohN (n)ah pahN-say)*	*he, she, one thought*
Nous avons pensé	*(noo zahvohN pahN-say)*	*we thought*
Vous avez pensé	*(voo zahvay pahN-say)*	*you thought*
Ils, elles ont pensé	*(eel, ehl zohN pahN-say)*	*they thought*

Some verbs use *être* (to be) to form the *passé composé*. Many words that express motion are used with *être*, like *aller* (to go), *arriver* (to arrive), and *venir* (to come). In the dialog in this chapter Monique said, *Je suis allée.* (I went.)

Notice that if you are writing, the past participle must agree with the subject. If the subject is feminine like Monique add an –e (*Je suis allée.*) If the subject is plural, add an –s *Nous sommes allés.* (We went.) If "we" refers to women and/or girls only, then it would be *Nous sommes allées.* (with that extra "e".)

So, the past participles of *être* act a little like adjectives since they agree in number and gender: For example:

MASCULINE SINGULAR   il est allé

FEMININE SINGULAR   elle est allée

MASCULINE PLURAL   ils sont allés

FEMININE PLURAL   elles sont allées

If this sounds confusing, the good news is that when you *say* the following forms of *aller*, they have exactly the same pronunciation: *aller, allé, allée, allés, allées (ah-lay).*

```
                        (ah-lay)
                        ALLER  (passé composé)
                        to go

                    masculine forms

    Je suis allé                (zhuh swee zah-lay)          I went
    Tu es allé                  (tew eh zah-lay)             you went
    Il est allé                 (eel, eh tah-lay)            he went
    Nous sommes allés           (noo sohm zah-lay)           we went
    Vous êtes allés             (voo zeh tah-lay)            you went
    Ils sont allés              (eel sohN tah-lay)           they went
```

PRACTICE

Use the pictures to help you fill in the blanks with the passé composé. Choose a past participle verb from the list and *add the helping verb*. Remember to use the present tense of *avoir* (have) or *être* (be), then the past participle. Examples: *J'ai mangé.* ("I ate.") *Il est allé.* (He went.)

Choose one of these words to complete your passé composé verbs.

nagé	allé	mangé	téléphoné
regardé	joué	parlé	pensé

Hier, j' _____ à mon amie.
                    1.

Nous _____ beaucoup du week end.
            2.

74

Elle était très fatiguée samedi parce

qu'elle _____ au foot toute la matinée.

3.

(reh-stay zheh zehl)

Alors, elle est restée chez elle le dimanche

stayed   at home

et _____ la télé toute la journée.

4.

Puis, elle m'a demandé "Qu'est–ce que tu as fait?" Je lui ai dit

(lahk)

que le samedi mon petit ami et moi _____ dans le lac.

5. *(Just guess!)*   *lake*

(boom)

Samedi soir nous _____ à une boum.

6.   *party*

CHAPTER 13

(kehs kuh tew vuh mahN-zhay)
Qu'est–ce que tu veux manger?
What do you want to eat?

zhay ewn faN duh loo
J'ai une faim de loup
I'm as hungry as a horse.

ah vohtr sahN-tay
A votre santé!
Cheers!

bohN ah-pay-tee
Bon appétit!
Have a good meal!

VOCABULARY

(luh tay)
le thé
tea

(luh leh)
le lait
milk

(luh kah-fay)
le café
coffee

(luh vaN)
le vin
wine

(lah bee-yehr)
la bière
beer

(lay frew-ee)
les fruits(m)
fruit

(lah-nah-nah)
l'ananas (m)
pineapple

(lah suh-reez)
la cerise
cherry

(luh day-sehr)
le dessert
dessert

(luh gah-to)
le gâteau
cake

(lah pohm)
la pomme
apple

(la frehz)
la fraise
strawberry

(loh-nyohN)
l'oignon
onion

(lah glahs)
la glace
ice cream

(lah tahrt)
la tarte
pie

(lah bah-nahn)
la banane
banana

(luh paN)
le pain
bread

(luh ree)
le riz
rice

(loh-rahNzh)
l'orange (f)
orange

(lay freet)
les frites
French fries

(lah vee-ahNd)
la viande
meat

(luh poo-leh)
le poulet
chicken

(lah kah-roht)
la carotte
carrot

(luh buhf)
le boeuf
beef

(luh shahN-pee-nyohN)
le champignon
mushroom

(luh jahN-bohN)
le jambon
ham

(lah toh-maht)
la tomate
tomato

(lah soop)
la soupe
soup

(luh froh-mazh)
le fromage
cheese

(lay lay-gewm)
les légumes
vegetables

(lah sah-lahd)
la salade
salad

STORY

(trwah zah-mee sohN dahN zuhN reh-stoh-rahN) (ahN-ree, greh-gwahr, ay-reek)
Trois amis sont dans un restaurant: Henri, Grégoire, Eric

(keh-skuh)   (voo voo-lay   mahN-zhay)
Henri: Qu'est–ce que vous voulez manger?
What do you want to eat?

(nay pah)   (soop)   (sah-lahd)
Grégoire: Je n'ai pas très faim. Je prends une soupe et une salade.

(twah)
Henri: Et toi, Eric?

(mahN-zhay)   (suh mah-taN)
Eric: Moi? J'ai une faim de loup. Je n'ai pas mangé de petit déjeuner ce matin.
this morning

(sehr-vuhr) (keh-skuh)   (voo day-zee-ray)
Le serveur: Qu'est–ce que vous désirez?

(zhuh prahN)   (ewn sah-land vehrt)
Grégoire: Je prends de la soupe et une salade verte.

(bohN) (poor)   (muh-syuh)
Le serveur: Bon. Pour vous, monsieur?

(ew noh-mleh to froh-mazh)
Henri: Moi, je voudrais une omelette au fromage et une salade de tomates.

(kwa dotr)
Le serveur: Quoi d'autre?
something else

Henri: Oui. S'il vous plaît, comme dessert *(kohm deh-sehr)* je voudrais de la tarte aux pommes.

Le serveur: Et vous, monsieur? *(ay voo)*

Eric: D'abord *(dah-bohrd)*, je voudrais des escargots *(day zehs-kahr-go)* en entrée *(ahN-treh)*. Ensuite...du poulet *(dew poo-lay)* à la moutarde *(moo-tahrd)*.

Comme dessert, je prends de la crème caramel *(krehm kah-rah-mehl)*, s'il vous plaît.

Le serveur: Je suis désolé *(zhuh swee)(day-zo-lay)*, monsieur. Nous n'avons plus de poulet *(noo nah-vohN plew)*. Nous avons un très
am   sorry   have no more

bon saumon servi avec une sauce au citron. *(so-mohN sehr-vee ah-veh-kewn so so see-trohN)*
salmon   lemon

Eric: D'accord *(dah-kohr)*. Je prends le saumon.   **Le Serveur:** Vous voulez un dessert? *(voo voo-lay uhN day-sehr)*

Eric: Oui. Je voudrais de la glace à la vanille *(glah sah lah vah-nee-y)*.   **Le Serveur:** Comme boisson? *(bwa-sohN)*
drink

Henri: Nous prenons une carafe de blanc *(kah-rahf duh blahN)*, s'il vous plaît.
a carafe of white wine

Le Serveur: Excellent. *(ehk-say-lahN)*

Henri, Grégoire, et Eric: A votre santé! Bon appétit!

PRACTICE

FOOD VOCABULARY

Use the clues in English to find the words *en français.*

ACROSS

3. cake
5. wine
7. cheese
8. fish

Down

1. mushroom
2. ham
4. ice cream
6. milk
7. strawberry

REVIEW

(vreh oo fo)
Comprenez–vous?: Vrai ou faux
true or false

1. Eric a très faim. _____

2. La tarte à la pomme est un dessert. _____

3. Henri a commandé du vin rouge. _____

4. Eric mange du poulet. _____

5. Eric veut de la glace au chocolat. _____

FOCUS: GRAMMAR

SOME, ANY

When speaking about food, you will want to use "some". You say *J'aime la glace* (I like ice cream), but *Je voudrais <u>de la</u> glace* (I would like some ice cream.) See the chart below to see the different forms of "some" that you use before the noun.

de + le = du *(dew)*	du fromage *(dew froh-mazh)*	some cheese
de + la = de la *(duh lah)*	de la salade *(duh lah sah-lahd)*	some salad
de + les = des *(day)*	des fraises *(day frehz)*	some strawberries
de + l' = de l' *(duhl)*	de l'eau *(duh lo)*	some water

If you want to say that you DON'T want something, just use *de* (which means "any" in a negative sentence). *Je ne veux pas <u>de</u> dessert.* (I don't want any dessert.)

CHAPTER 14

(keh-skuh tew ah)
Qu'est–ce que tu as?
What's the matter? What's wrong?

(zhuh swee kruh-vay)
Je suis crevée
I'm exhausted.

(zhwah-yuh zah-nee-vehr-sehr)
Joyeux anniversaire!
Happy Birthday!

(keh-skuh tew ah)
Qu'est–ce que tu as?
What's the matter?

(zhuh muh sahN mahl)
Je me sens mal.
I feel sick.

VOCABULARY

(feh-tay)
fêter
to celebrate

(uhN rewm)
un rhume
a cold

(mah-lahd)
malade
sick/ill

(lah sahN-tay)
la santé
health

(pwah)
poids
weight

(uhN vay-lo)
un vélo
a bicycle

(luh zhahr-daN)
le jardin
the garden

(uhN vehr)
un verre
a glass

DIALOG

(trwah zah-mee suh ruh-troov   sheh)
Trois amies se retrouvent chez Sarah pour déjeuner et fêter l'anniversaire de Christine.
        meet   at the home of

Sarah: Salut, Christine! Joyeux anniversaire!

Christine: Salut, Sarah! Merci! Quel jour magnifique, aujourd'hui! On va déjeuner dehors?
                        (kehl)   (mah-nyee-feek)   (ohN)   (dohr)
                                                                                we   outside

Sarah: Oui, dans le jardin...Julie, qu'est-ce que tu as?

Julie: Je me sens mal.

Sarah: Quel dommage! As-tu un rhume?
(kehl doh-mazh)
too bad

Julie: Je pense que oui. J'ai mal à la
(zhuh pahNs kuh wee)
I think so

gorge et je suis crevée.

Sarah: Depuis combien de temps es-tu malade?
(duh-pew-ee ko-byaN duh tahN eh-tew mah-lahd)
how long have you been sick

Julie: Depuis environ deux jours.
(ahN-vee-rohN)
for about

Sarah: Pourquoi es-tu venue?
(poor-kwah eh-tew vuh-new)
why   did you come

Julie: C'est l'anniversaire de Christine! Je veux participer à la fête!
                                        (pahr-tee-see-pay)

Christine: C'est si gentil de ta part, Julie. Merci.
(seh see zhahN-tee)   (pahr)
so nice of you

Julie: *(dah-yehr)* D'ailleurs, comment vas–tu, Christine? Tu étais si malade le mois dernier. *(mwah dehr-nyay)*
anyway *last month*

Christine: *(veh)* Je vais bien *(maN-tnahN)* maintenant. *(ruh-gahrd mwah)* Regarde–moi! J'ai pris un peu de poids. *(pree uhN puh duh pwah)*
now *look* *gained a little weight*

Julie: *(seh fahN-tah-steek)* C'est fantastique. Tu as l'air en pleine forme! *(leh rahN plehn fohrm)* Comment va ton travail? *(ko-mahN)*
you look great

Christine: *(day-bohr-day)* Je suis débordée, mais c'est très intéressant.
swamped

(rahN-kohNtr shahk) Je rencontre chaque jour des gens *(zhahN)* différents. *(dee-fay-rahN)*
meet *people*

Julie: *(shweht)* Chouette!
great

Sarah: *(ah tahbl)* A table! On va manger de la salade niçoise, de l'ananas, du pain, du *(nee-swahz)*
to the table   *we are going to eat*

fromage, et un gâteau au chocolat comme dessert. Commençons avec un verre de champagne. *(o shoh-co-lah kohm)*   *(koh-mahN-sohN)*   *(vehr shahN-pah- nyuh)*
                                              glass

J,C,S: *(ah vohtr sahN-tay)* A votre santé!
      to your health (cheers)

Julie et Sarah: *(kah-rahN-tyehm)* Au quarantième anniversaire de Christine!

Christine: *(sewr-too)* Et à la santé surtout de Julie!
             especially

Julie: *(day-zhah mee-yuh)* Je me sens déjà mieux!
     I feel better already!

OUI OU NON?

Read *en anglais*. Answer *en français*.

_____ 1. Does Julie have a sore throat?

_____ 2. Does Christine like her job?

_____ 3. Is the celebration at Julie's house?

_____ 4. Is it Christine's thirtieth birthday?

_____ 5. Was Christine sick last month?

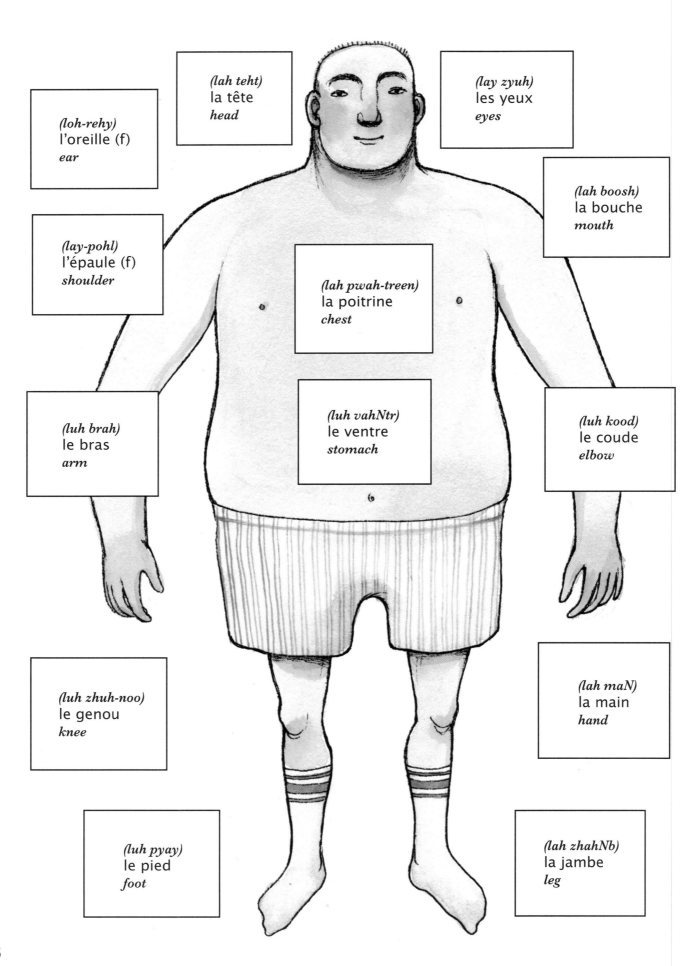

(loh-rehy)
l'oreille (f)
ear

(lah teht)
la tête
head

(lay zyuh)
les yeux
eyes

(lah boosh)
la bouche
mouth

(lay-pohl)
l'épaule (f)
shoulder

(lah pwah-treen)
la poitrine
chest

(luh brah)
le bras
arm

(luh vahNtr)
le ventre
stomach

(luh kood)
le coude
elbow

(luh zhuh-noo)
le genou
knee

(lah maN)
la main
hand

(luh pyay)
le pied
foot

(lah zhahNb)
la jambe
leg

86

PRACTICE

(keh-skuh voo zah-vay)
Qu'est-ce que vous avez?
What's the matter? (formal)

If you happen to get hurt or sick while you're in a French-speaking country, here's how you can tell someone what hurts or bothers you: use *avoir mal à* + the definite article + the body part = *J'ai mal aux dents.* (My teeth hurt.)

Remember that Julie said, *"J'ai mal à la gorge."* (I have a sore throat.) See if you can match *l'anglais with le français* by looking at the diagram. Write the letters in the blanks.

1. J'ai mal au ventre.   _____   a. My feet hurt.
2. J'ai mal au genou.   _____   b. My eyes hurt.
3. J'ai mal à la tête.   _____   c. I have a stomachache.
4. J'ai mal aux pieds.   _____   d. My back hurts.
5. J'ai mal à l'oreille.   _____   e. My neck hurts.
6. J'ai mal aux yeux.   _____   f. My knee hurts.
7. J'ai mal au cou.   _____   g. I have a headache.
8. J'ai mal au dos.   _____   h. I have an earache.

You may remember that in Chapter 11 Sami *le chien* can *sentir* the good food in the oven. *Sentir* means "to smell", but when this verb becomes reflexive *(se sentir)*, it means "to feel". Reflexive just means that you perform an action upon yourself. You can recognize a reflexive verb by the reflexive pronouns that come right before the verb (unlike in English where the reflexive pronoun comes <u>after</u> the verb- I wash <u>myself</u>.)

You've seen this type of verb already with *Je m'appelle...* (My name is....) Literally it means "I call myself". *Je me brosse les dents (zhuh muh brohs lay dahN)* means "I brush my teeth." *Je me sens bien (zhuh muh sahN byaN)* = I feel good. *Je me sens mal* = I feel bad (sick).

(suh sahN-teer)
SE SENTIR
to feel

je me sens	*(zhuh muh sahN)*	*I feel*
tu te sens	*(tew tuh sahN)*	*you feel*
il, elle, on se sent	*(eel, ehl, ohN suh sahN)*	*he, she, one feels*
nous nous sentons	*(noo noo sahN-tohN)*	*we feel*
vous vous sentez	*(voo voo sahN-tay)*	*you feel*
ils, elles se sentent	*(eel, ehl suh sahNt)*	*they feel*

CHAPTER 15

(sah tuh vah ah mehr-vay-y)
Ça te va à merveille!
That looks great on you!

(zhah-meh duh lah vee)
Jamais de la vie!
No way!

(nuh tahN feh pah)
Ne t'en fais pas.
Don't worry.

(ahN sohld)
en solde
on sale

VOCABULARY

(luh mah-yo duh baN)
le maillot de bain
swimsuit

(luh kohs-tewm)
le costume
suit

(lay sho-seht)
les chaussettes(f)
socks

(luh pewl)
le pull
pullover

(lay-shahrp)
l'écharpe(f)
scarf (long)

(luh zheen)
le jean
jeans

(lah rohb)
la robe
dress

(luh koh-lahN)
le collant
tights

(luh shohrt)
le short
shorts

(luh foo-lahr)
le foulard
scarf

(luh shah-po)
le chapeau
hat

(lah vehst)
la veste
jacket

(laN-pehr-may-ahbl)
l'imperméable(m)
raincoat

(lah shuh-meez)
la chemise
shirt

(luh shuh-meez-yay)
le chemisier
blouse

(lah krah-vaht)
la cravate
tie

(lah saN-tewr)
la ceinture
belt

(luh pah-rah-plew-ee)
le parapluie
umbrella

(lah jewp)
la jupe
skirt

(luh pahN-tah-lohN)
le pantalon
pants

(lay boht)
les bottes (f)
boots

(lay sho-sewr)
les chaussures(f)
shoes

DIALOG

(mee-shehl ay mah-ree mahr-taN pahrt ahN vwah-yazh dah-fehr ah ah-wa-yi)   *(traN dahsh-tay)*
Michel et Marie Martin partent en voyage d'affaires à Hawaï. Ils sont en train d'acheter
               are leaving   *business trip*   *in the process of buying*

(day veht-mahN)   *(mahn-tnahN)*   *(mah-gah-zaN)*   *(poo rohm)*
des vêtements. Ils sont maintenant dans un magasin de vêtements pour hommes.
   clothes   *now*   *store*

        (eh-say)   *(gree)*
Michel essaie un costume gris.
      is trying on

        (suh)   *(tuh vah byaN)*   *(zhuh nuh veh pah zahN-pohr-tay)*
Marie: Ce costume te va bien, mais je ne vais pas emporter un costume.
        this   *fits you well*   *bring*

        (tew ah puh teht reh-zohN)   *(troh pa-bee-yay)*   *(day ray-ewnyohN ah ah-wa-yi)*
Michel: Tu as peut–être raison. C'est trop habillé pour des réunions à Hawaï.
      perhaps you're right   *It's too dressy for*   *meetings*

        (meh suh pahN-tah-lohn ay seht)
Marie: Mets ce pantalon et cette chemise rose.
     put on these pants   *this*

Michel: Rose? Jamais de la vie!

(dohn)
Donne–moi une chemise bleue, s'il te plaît.
give

        (pwee-zhuh voo zay-day)
Vendeur: Puis–je vous aider?
     can I help you

Michel: Avez–vous cette chemise en bleu?

        (mehm tah-y)
Vendeur: La même taille?
     the same size

Michel: Oui.

        (lah vwa-see)
Vendeur: La voici.
     here it is

Michel: *(seh myuh)* C'est mieux. Je cherche aussi une veste de sport. *(shehrsh o-see) (ewn vehs duh spohr)*
that's better   *am looking for*   *sport jacket*

Vendeur: *(sehl-see eh tahN)* Celle-ci est en solde.
this one

Marie: *(seh treh zay-lay-gahN) (sa tuh vah sew-pehr byaN shay-ree)* C'est très élégant. Ça te va super bien, Chéri!
that fits you really well, dear

Michel: *(byaN zhah-sheht)* Bien. J'achète le pantalon, la chemise et la veste.

Vendeur: *(pay-yay) (kehs lah-bah)* Merci de payer à la caisse là-bas.
at cash register over there

Michel et Marie sont maintenant dans un magasin de vêtements pour femmes. Marie essaie une robe jaune.

Michel: *(zhoh-lee)* Cette robe est jolie, mais elle est trop longue. *(troh lohNg)*
pretty   *too*   *long*

Marie: Peut-être... Mademoiselle, avez-vous la taille en dessous pour cette robe? *(ahN deh-soo)*
a size smaller

Vendeuse: Non, madame, nous n'avons pas cette taille.

Michel: Regarde cette robe rouge, Chérie.

Marie: Cette robe est laide. Je ne peux pas mettre ça.
(lehd) ugly   *(nuh puh pah mehtr sa)* I can't put that on

Michel: Ne t'en fais pas. Je ne l'aime pas non plus!
it *either*

Vendeuse: Est-ce que cette jupe vous plaît, madame? C'est la dernière et elle est à votre taille.
(eh skuh) *(seht)*   *(pleh)* please you   *(dehr-nee-ehr)* last one   your size

Marie: Cette jupe me plaît beaucoup! **Michel:** Essaie-la!
(seht) *(muh)* me   *(eh-say lah)*

Vendeuse: Voici un chemisier jaune et une écharpe de soie à mettre avec la jupe.
(swah ah meh trah-vek) silk   to put on with

Marie: OK....Qu'est-ce que tu en penses? **Michel:** Ça te va à merveille!
(keh-skuh tew ahN pahNs)

Marie: Parfait! Allons voir les maillots de bains. Ensuite, nous serons prêts pour Hawaï.
(pahr-feh) let's go see   *(ahN-sweet)* then   *(seh-rohN preh)* we'll be ready

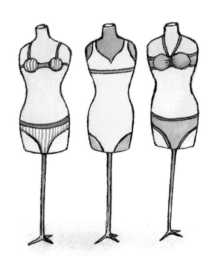

DO YOU UNDERSTAND?

Which of these statements describe the situations in the dialogs? Put a check next to the sentences that are true.

1. _____ Michel achète une chemise rose.

2. _____ Marie aime la jupe.

3. _____ Michel essaie un imperméable.

4. _____ Michel et Marie vont à Hawaï.

Each of the 5 words below is a scrambled word for a piece of women's clothing. Unscramble each of the clue words. Copy the letters in the numbered cells to other cells with the same number. Then you will find the answer to the question! (The answer does not refer to the dialogs in this chapter. This is just to practice some of the new words you learned.)

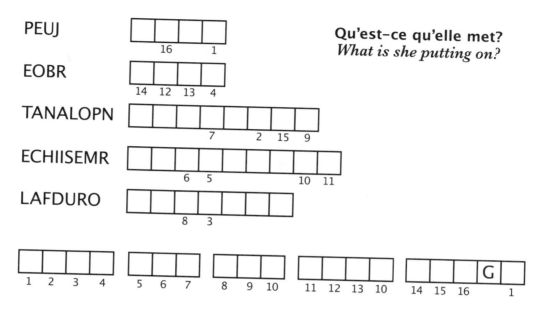

PEUJ

☐☐☐☐
16　　1

EOBR

☐☐☐☐
14 12 13 4

TANALOPN

☐☐☐☐☐☐☐☐
　　　7　　2 15 9

ECHIISEMR

☐☐☐☐☐☐☐☐☐
　　6 5　　　10 11

LAFDURO

☐☐☐☐☐☐☐
　　　8 3

Qu'est–ce qu'elle met?
What is she putting on?

☐☐☐☐　☐☐☐　☐☐☐　☐☐☐☐　☐☐G☐
1 2 3 4　5 6 7　8 9 10　11 12 13 10　14 15 16　1

You saw some ways to say "this" in the dialog: *ce costume, ce pantalon, cette robe, cette jupe*. These are adjectives (demonstrative adjectives) so they must agree in gender and number with the noun they modify:

	SINGULAR			PLURAL		
Masculine	ce/cet*	(suh/seht)	this/that	ces	(say)	these/those
Feminine	cette	(seht)	this/that	ces	(say)	these/those

FOCUS

THIS, THAT, THESE, THOSE

In the dialog, you also saw *celle-ci (sehl-see)* which means "this one". "That one" in this case would be *celle-là (sehl-lah)*. These are forms of demonstrative pronouns that must also agree in gender and number with the nouns they refer to. (Notice that French demonstrative pronouns are different from demonstrative adjectives, unlike English.) Take a look at the chart:

	SINGULAR		PLURAL	
	this one	that one	these ones	those ones
Masculine	celui *(suhlwee)*-ci	celui-là	ceux *(suh)*-ci	ceux-là
Feminine	celle *(sehl)*-ci	celle-là	celles *(sehl)*-ci	celles-là

*Use this in front of a masculine noun that starts with a vowel:　*(seh-taN-pehr-may-ahbl)*
cet impermeable

CHAPTER 16

(seh lah vee)
C'est la vie!
That's life!

No matter how much *vous* prepare for *un voyage* to a foreign country, there will often be some unexpected things that can happen. When some of these things are unfortunate or unpleasant, it helps to know some of *la langue* in order *comprendre* what people (like *les docteurs* or *les agents de police*) are asking. *Vous* might *aussi* need *expliquer* what happened. A good attitude goes a long way in preparing *vous* to cope with unfortunate circumstances. Accepting an unforeseen event as part of *votre* experience will help you get through it. You will see in the story in this chapter how Robert, from New York, handles *ses problèmes* on a business trip to Marseilles.

(kehl oh-ruhr)
Quelle horreur!
What a terrible thing!

(myuh vo tahr kuh zhah-meh)
Mieux vaut tard que jamais!
Better late than never!

VOCABULARY

(lay-krahN)
l'écran
screen

(luh pohr-tabl)
le portable (m)
laptop computer

(laN-pree-mahNt)
l'imprimante
printer

(luh ray-pohN-duhr)
le répondeur
answering machine

(lohr-dee-nah-tuhr)
l'ordinateur (m)
computer

(luh fahks)
le fax
fax machine

(luh tay-lay-fohn pohr-tahbl)
(le téléphone) portable
cell phone

(luh klah-vyay)
le clavier
keyboard

(lah soo-ree)
la souris
mouse

(suh kee eh tah-ree-vay)   *(vwah-yah zhah mahr-say-y)*
Read *ce qui est arrivé* to Robert on a *voyage à Marseilles.*
    what happened

                 (shahNs)   *(dah-fehr)*
Mon frère Robert n'a pas de chance. Il est allé en voyage d'affaires à Marseille le mois
              is not lucky   *went*   *business trip*

                                 (voh-lay) *(lah-ay-ro-pohr)*
dernier. D'abord, son ordinateur portable a été volé dans l'aéroport. Quelle horreur!
                                     was stolen   *airport*

(ahNsweet)   *(eh-say-yay dahN-vwah-yay)*   *(bew-ro)*   *(pah-trohN)*
Ensuite, il a essayé d'envoyer un fax à son bureau de New York, mais son patron ne l'a
        tried to send   *office*   *his* *boss* *it*

   (reh-sew)   *(suh-lah)*   *(ew-tee-lee-zay)*   *(leh-say)*   *(meh-sahzh)*
pas reçu. Après cela, Robert a utilisé son téléphone portable pour laisser un message sur
         that   *used*   *leave*

             (mahr-sheh)
le répondeur du travail, mais il ne marchait pas. Quelle horreur!
         wasn't working

    (swee-vahN) *(eh tah-ree-vay)*   *(treh zay-nehr-vay)*
Le jour suivant, il est arrivé à Marseille. Robert était très énervé parce qu'il s'était
   following   *annoyed* *because*

(pehr-dew)   *(rahN-day-voo)*
perdu et était en retard de 40 minutes sur son premier rendez–vous.
lost   *meeting*

      (kehl-kaN)   *(sahl lew-ee ah dee)*
(Quand quelqu'un dans la salle lui a dit "Mieux vaut tard que jamais!" D'abord il n'a
when someone   *room* *said to him*

  (kohN-pree luh sahNs) *(ah-preh zah-vwahr)* *(seh sahN-tee)*
pas compris le sens. Après avoir compris, il s'est senti un peu mieux.)
didn't understand the meaning *after having*   *felt*   *better*

(ray-ew-see ah ahN-vwah-yay   say zee-mehl)   *(kehl-kuh zah-mee)*
Robert a réussi à envoyer ses emails à son patron, sa famille, et à quelques amis. Il a
  succeeded   *some*

(troo-vay)   *(aN-tehr-neht)*   *(ew-tee-leez luhr zohr-dee-nah-tuhr) (prehsk)*
trouvé un café Internet pas loin de son hôtel. Il utilise leurs ordinateurs presque chaque
found   *their*   *almost*

        (mohN frehr)   *(kee-lee-ah-veh too-zjoor)*   *(bo-koo dmohNd)*
soir. Mon frère Robert m'a dit qu'il y avait toujours beaucoup de monde au café Internet
                                     me   that there were always   *lots of people*

(ahN-vwah-yahN)   *(sewr-fahN)*   *(wehb)*   *(ew-tee-lee-zahN luh treht-mahN duh tehxt)*
envoyant des emails, surfant sur le Web, et utilisant le traitement de texte.
sending   *word processor*

(suh-pahN-dahN)   *(tah-pay)*   *(klah-vyay)*
Cependant, Robert n'a pas réussi à taper très vite, parce que le clavier est différent.
however   *to type*   *keyboard*

        (rahN-vehr-say)
Un soir, il a renversé du café sur la souris et sur le clavier. Le propriétaire n'était pas du
      spilled   *owner*   *wasn't at all*

tout content. Quelle horreur!

Ensuite, le samedi, par un matin ensoleillé, Robert a loué une voiture pour aller à la
(ahN-soh-lehy) *(loo-ay)*
rented

campagne faire un pique–nique au bord de la rivière. Malheureusement, sa
(kah-pah-nyuh fehr uhN pee-kneek o bohr) *(ree-vyehr mah-luh-ruhz-mahN)*
country *edge* *unfortunately*

voiture est tombée en panne sur l'autoroute. Quelle horreur!
(tohN-bay ahN pahn) *(loto-root)*
broke down *highway*

Le dimanche, il a loué un vélo pour aller dans un grand parc. Il a plu presque tout le
(vay-lo) *(grahN pahrk)* *(plew)*
bicycle *it rained*

temps et son pneu s'était dégonflé sur le chemin du retour.
(pnuh) *(day-gohN-flay)* *(shuh-maN)* *(ruh-toor)*
got a flat tire *road* *return*

Quelle horreur!

Pauvre Robert! Cependant, même quand
(povr) *(mehm)*
poor *even*

il n'a pas de chance, mon
he's not lucky

frère est optimiste et dit
(ohp-tee-meest)

toujours "C'est la vie!"

DO YOU UNDERSTAND?

_____ 1. "Mieux vaut tard que jamais!"   a) la souris et le clavier

_____ 2. le patron n'a pas reçu   b) café Internet

_____ 3. est tombée en panne sur l'autoroute   c) au rendez–vous

_____ 4. a renversé du café sur   d) l'ordinateur portable

_____ 5. le pneu s'était dégonflé   e) la voiture

_____ 6. il a envoyé ses emails du   f) le vélo

_____ 7. était volé   g) un fax

MATCHING

See if you can match the past tense verb with the meaning. Look back at the story for help.

1. trouvé   _____   a) rented

2. loué   _____   b) stolen

3. perdu   _____   c) tried

4. compris   _____   d) found

5. reçu   _____   e) lost

6. arrivé   _____   f) understood

7. volé   _____   g) arrived

8. renversé   _____   h) received

9. essayé   _____   i) spilled

FOCUS

If you are involved in any kind of accident or are the victim of a theft or an attack, you need some language to help you communicate. Try to get help from **_un agent de police (ah-zhahN duh po-lees)_** or **_un gendarme (zhahN-dahrm)_**– both are words for police officer. Emergency phone numbers are usually listed on the first page of the telephone directory (just like in the U.S.). Always fill out a report and get a hold of the American consulate if you need help: **_Je dois contacter le consultat (zhuh dwah kohN-tahk-tay luh kohN-sew-lah)_** – I have to contact the consulate.

(ewr-zhahNs)
urgence
emergency

(ah lehd)
A l'aide!
Help!

(voh-luhr)
Voleur!
Thief!

(poh-lees)
Police!
Police!

(keh-skee seh pah-say)
Qu'est–ce qui s'est passé?
What happened?

(ohN mah voh-lay)
On m'a volé
They stole my…

(zhuh vuh seen-ya-lay)
Je veux signaler
I want to report

(ah-puh-lay lay pohN-pyeh)
Appelez les pompiers!
Call the fire department!

FOCUS

Find these 4 emergency words in the puzzle: *feu, police, urgence, voleur.* Then circle them.

r	v	f	d	a	x	a	w	u	g
g	w	o	e	l	f	e	k	r	o
i	t	b	l	u	s	z	o	g	w
v	f	x	s	e	u	q	l	e	t
s	u	s	j	y	u	q	i	n	t
q	i	z	x	t	w	r	g	c	i
d	p	o	l	i	c	e	u	e	g

Be sure to use the accompanying "phrase" stickers to practice what you've learned. Place them around your work and home. Build on the foundation this book provides by immersing yourself in French as much as you can. French radio and television programs may be available in your area. French films are another enjoyable way to hear the language. Read anything you can find in French, including children's books, easy novels, comics, magazines, newspapers, and even the labels on household products. Search the Internet for French websites that will give you countless opportunities to read and listen to French.

ANSWER KEY

CHAPTER 1

Practice *p.8*

1. Où <u>veux</u>-tu prendre <u>le dîner</u>?
2. Où veux-tu <u>prendre le déjeuner</u>?
3. <u>Où</u> veux-tu prendre <u>le petit déjeuner?</u>
4. <u>Où</u> veux-tu aller?

Matching *p.9*

1. E   2. A   3. D   4. B   5. C   6. F

CHAPTER 2

Number Practice *p.13*

1. quatre   2. dix   3. cinq   4. trois
5. un   6. sept   7. huit   8. neuf

Practice *p.15*

1. Anne et son amie mangent dans <u>un café.</u>
2. Julie a <u>deux</u> sandwichs.
3. Jacques <u>entre</u> dans le cafe.
4. Jacques <u>est très content</u>.

CHAPTER 3

Practice *p.19*

1. Quel âge as-tu?   2. D'où venez-vous?
3. Comment vous appelez-vous?   4. Vous êtes américain?

Practice – Asking Questions in French *p.20*

1. Est-ce que vous êtes français?   2. Tu as faim?
3. Est-ce que vous avez faim?   4. D'où venez-vous?
5. Mangez-vous les escargots?   6. Vous avez quel âge?

CHAPTER 4

Do You Understand? *p.25*

1. Isabelle   2. Il parle un peu français. (He speaks a little french.)

3. deux éclairs au chocolat (two chocolate eclairs)   4. Isabelle
5. dans une boulangerie (in a bakery)

Practice: What would you like? *p.27*

1. onze   2. dix-huit   3. quinze
4. trois   5. cinq   6. deux

CHAPTER 5

Practice *p.31*

1. house(maison)   2. years old (ans)   3. nice (sympathique)
4. funny (marrante) 5. work/job (travail) 6. train (train)   7. car (voiture)

Crossword Puzzle: Colors *p.32*

Across: 3. rouge 6. gris 7. marron 8. vert
Down: 1. jaune 2. bleu 3. rose 4. orange 5. blanc

Practice: Days of the Week *p.33*

3 mercredi   7 dimanche   2 mardi   5 vendredi   1 lundi   6 samedi   4 jeudi

CHAPTER 6

Practice: Ordinal Number *p.37*

A is premier   F is sixième
B is deuxième   G is septième
C is troisième   H is huitième
D is quatrième   I is neuvième
E is cinquième   J is dixième

Practice: Comprenez-vous? *p.39*

1. non   2. oui   3. non   4. non

CHAPTER 7

Practice: Translating picture captions *p.42*

1. The mother is at the beach during the summer.
2. The father is in the mountains during the winter.
3. The brother is hiking during the autumn.
4. The sisters are looking at the flowers in the spring.

Practice: Translating story sentences *p.44*

A. French to English

1. My father prefers winter.
2. My brother, Robert, who is 17, likes to hike in the forest.
3. When do we take our vacation?
4. From time to time, we also hike in the winter and spring.

B. English to French

1. J'ai vingt (20) ans.
2. Il aime les couleurs de l'automne (orange, rouge, jaune, marron).
3. Moi aussi! Janine et moi aimons les belles fleurs.
4. En juin, juillet et août nous allons souvent à la plage.

Focus: Definite Articles – Noun Gender Practice *p.45*

1. la soeur	2. la plage	3. la famille	4. le fromage
5. la voiture	6. l'homme	7. le matin	8. la saison
9. le musée	10. la rue		

CHAPTER 8

Practice: Family Members *p.49*

1. a) Patrick b) le frère   2. a) Morgane b) la belle-soeur   3. a) René b) le père

4. a) Sophie b) la mère   5. a) Andrée b) la femme

6. a) Hélène b) la belle-mère   7. a) Albert b) le beau-père   8. a) Nathalie b) la fille

Questions: *p.50*   1. Andrée 2. Sophie 3. Patrick 4. Nathalie 5. Pierre

Focus: Adjectives *p.50*

1. la grande femme	2. la petite fille	3. le beau mari
4. la belle grand-mère	5. la nièce intelligente	6. les pères intelligents

Practice: Possessive Adjectives *p.51*

1. ma	2. ma	3. son	4. ta	5. leurs
6. votre	7. mes	8. leur	9. sa	10. nos

CHAPTER 9

Practice: Comprenez-vous? *p.55*

1. Elise
2. en Alaska
3. à Paris
4. tous les jours sauf le dimanche (du lundi au samedi)

Matching *p.55*

Elise (la fille)	Maman
2, 3, 5, 7, 8	1, 4, 6

Practice – Quel temps fait-il? *p.56*

1. il fait chaud
2. il pleut beaucoup
3. il fait mauvais
4. il neige
5. il y a du vent
6. il fait humide
7. il fait beau

Practice and Review *p.57*

1. neige
2. froid
3. beaucoup
4. ici
5. printemps

CHAPTER 10

Do You Understand? *p.61*

1. F   2. T   3. F   4. F   5. T

Practice: Time *p.62*

1. d   2. e   3. a   4. c   5. b

CHAPTER 11

Do You Understand? *p.68*

1. D   2. C   3. E   4. B   5. A

Practice: Prepositions *p.69*

1. dans
2. sur
3. sur
4. derrière
5. sous
6. à côté

Write Two Sentences

Possible answers:
1. Il y a un livre sur le tapis.
2. Le chien est à côté du lit.
3. Le chien est sur le tapis.
4. Le livre est par terre.
5. Les jouets sont par terre.

CHAPTER 12

Matching *p.72*

1. c   2. a   3. b   4. e   5. f   6. d

Practice: Passé composé *p.74*

1. ai téléphoné	2. avons parlé	3. a joué
4. a regardé	5. avons nagé	6. sommes allés

CHAPTER 13

Practice: Food Vocabulary Crossword *p.80*

Across: 3. gâteau 5. vin 7. fromage 8. poisson
Down: 1. champignon 2. jambon 4. glace 6. lait 7. fraise

Review: Vrai ou faux *p.81*

1. vrai–T   2. vrai –T   3. faux–F (vin blanc)   4. faux–F (saumon)
5. faux–F (glace à la vanille)

CHAPTER 14

Oui ou non? *p.85*

1. oui   2. oui   3. non (chez Christine)   4. non (40th)   5. oui

Practice: Qu'est-ce que vous avez? *p.87*

1. c   2. f   3. g   4. a   5. h   6. b   7. e   8. d

CHAPTER 15

Do You Understand? *p.92*

1. F   2. T   3. F   4. T

Word Scramble: Clothing *p.93*

PEUJ = jupe   EOBR = robe   TANALOPN = pantalon
ECHIISEMER = chemisier   LAFDURO = foulard

Elle	met	une	robe	rouge
1 2 3 4	5 6 7	8 9 10	11 12 13 10	14 15 16 1

CHAPTER 16

Do You Understand? *p.98*

1. c   2. g   3. e   4. a   5. f   6. b   7. d

Matching: Verbs *p.98*

1. d   2. a   3. e   4. f   5. h   6. g   7. b   8. i   9. c

GLOSSARY

The numbers after each entry indicate the chapter where the word first occurs or where there is more detailed information about that word.

m = masculine
f = feminine
pl = plural

FRENCH WORD	ENGLISH	CHAPTER
à	to, in, at	1
à côté de	next to	6
a votre santé	cheers	14
acheter	to buy	15
adorer	to adore, love	11
âge(m)	age	3
aider	to help	15
aimer	to like, love	5,11
aller	to go	1
alors	then	1
américain(m),américaine(f)	American	7
ami(m), amie(f)	friend	1
amusant(m),amusante (f)	amusing	12
ananas(m)	pineapple	13
anglais(m)	English	7
année(f)	year	7
anniversaire(m)	birthday	14
ans(m)	years	3
août(m)	August	7
après	after	9
après-midi(m)	afternoon	10
arriver	to arrive	10
artiste(m,f)	artist	2
assez	enough, quite	11
attendre	to wait for	5
au contraire	on the contrary	3
au revoir	goodbye	4
aujourd' hui	today	6
aussi	also	7
automne(m)	autumn	7
autre	other	7
avec	with	5
avion(m)	airplane	7
avis(m)	opinion	7
avoir	to have	3
avoir besoin de	to have need of	8
avoir raison	to be right	15
avril(m)	April	7
banque(f)	bank	6
beau(m),belle(f),beaux(pl)	beautiful	6
beaucoup	a lot	1
beau-père(m)	father-in-law	8
belle-mère(f)	mother-in-law	8
belle-soeur(f)	sister-in-law	8
bien	good, well	1
bien sûr	sure, of course	3
bière(f)	beer	13
billet(m)	ticket	4
blaguer	to joke	12
blanc(m), blanche(f)	white	5
bleu(m), bleue(f)	blue	5
boire	to drink	13
boisson(f)	drink(noun)	13
bon(m), bonne(f)	good	1
bonjour	hello,good morning	1
boulangerie (f)	bakery	4
boulevard(m)	boulevard	6
boum(f)	party	12
bouteille(f)	bottle	4
bras(m)	arm	14
bureau(m)	office, desk	16
c'est	it is	1
ça (cela)	it	1
café	coffee	4
café(m)	café	2
campagne(m)	countryside	4
cartes(f)	(playing) cards	11
carte postale(f)	postcard	4
ce(m), cette(f), ces(pl)	this	15
cependant	however	7
chaise(f)	chair	11
chambre(f)	bedroom	11

106

FRENCH WORD	ENGLISH	CHAPTER
champignon(m)	mushroom	13
chance(f)	luck	2
chapeau(m)	hat	8
chaque	each, every	5
chance(f)	luck	16
chat(m), chatte(f)	cat	11
chaud	hot	9
chéri(m), chérie (f)	dear	9
cheveux(m)	hair	8
chez	at (a place)	14
chien(m)	dog	6
chocolat(m)	chocolate	4
choisir	to choose	5
cinéma	cinema (movie theater)	6
cinq	five	2
cinquième	fifth	6
combien	how much	4
commencer	to begin	14
comment	how, what (did you say?)	3,10
comprendre	to understand	4
concert(m)	concert	10
confortable	comfortable	11
content(m), contente(f)	happy	2
copain(m), copine(f)	friend	13
corbeille à papier(f)	wastebasket	12
corps(m)	body	14
couleur(f)	color	7
course(f)	race	6
court(m), courte(f)	short	8
coûter	to cost	4
cravate(f)	necktie	7
cuisine(f)	kitchen	11
cuisiner	to cook	11
d'abord	at first	16
d'accord	OK, agreed	2
d'ailleurs	besides	12
dans	in	1
de l'autre côté de	on the other side of	6
de rien, je vous en prie	you're welcome	2
de, d'	from, to, of	4
décembre(m)	December	3
dedans	inside	11
dehors	outside	11
déjà	already	7
déjeuner(m)	lunch	1
demain	tomorrow	9
demander	to ask	1
demi(m), demie(f)	half	2
depuis	since	14
derrière	behind	10
des	some,	11
descendre	to go down	7
désirer	to desire, want	6,10
désolé	sorry	13
deux	two	4
deuxième	second	2
devant	in front of	11
devoir	to have to, must	6
dimanche(m)	Sunday	5
dîner(m)	dinner, to dine	16
dire	to say, tell	10
dix	ten	1
dix–huit	eighteen	2
dixième	tenth	4
dix–neuf	nineteen	6
dix–sept	seventeen	4
docteur(m)	doctor	4
doigt(m)	finger	14
donc	so	2
donner	to give	2
dormir	to sleep	11
douze	twelve	1
droit(m), droite(f)	right	4
dynamique	dynamic	6
eau minérale(f)	mineral water	7
elle	she, it	1
elles(f)	they	1
en	in, some	1
en avance	early	2
en bas	downstairs	10
en face de	facing	11

FRENCH WORD	ENGLISH	CHAPTER
en fait	in fact	6
en haut	upstairs	11
en retard	late	10
en train de	in the middle of doing something	2
encore	still	12
enfant(m)	child	8
ennuyeux(m), ennuyeuse(f)	boring	5
ensemble	together	5
ensuite	then, next	5
entrée(f)	first course	13
entrer	to enter	6
envoyer	to send	16
escargot(m)	snail	13
essayer	to try on	15
et	and	3
état(m)	state	3
été	summer	7
étoile(f)	star	5
étonnant	astonishing, surprising	10
être	to be	3
euro(m)	monetary unit of Europe	4
faim(m)	hunger	2
faire	to do	9
faire des courses	to go shopping	6
famille(f)	family	6
fatigué	tired	7
femme(f)	woman, wife	3,8
femme d'affaires(f)	businesswoman	8
fenêtre(f)	window	11
fermé	closed	6
fêter	celebrate	14
feu(m)	fire	16
février(m)	February	7
fille(f)	girl, daughter	3,8
fils(m)	son	8
finir	to finish	5
fleur(f)	flower	5
foot, football(m)	soccer	11
forêt(f)	forest	5
four(m)	oven	11
fraise(f)	strawberry	13
français(m)	French	7
frère(m)	brother	7
froid	cold	7
fromage(m)	cheese	13
gagner	to win	6
garçon(m)	boy	2
gare(f)	train station	10
gâteau(m)	cake	1
gauche	left	6
gendarme(m)	policeman	16
génial	great	6
gens(m)	people	14
glace(f)	ice cream	13
gorge(f)	throat	14
grand(m), grande(f)	big, tall	6
grand-père(m)	grandfather	5
grave	serious	8
gris	gray	3
habiter	to live	5
heure(f)	hour	10
hier	yesterday	9
hiver(m)	winter	7
homme(m)	man	1
hôtel(m)	hotel	5
huit	eight	2
huitième	eighth	6
humide	humid	1
ici	here	7
il	he, it	1
ils	they	1
il y a	there is, there are	7, 10
immédiatement	immediately	6
intelligent(m), intelligente(f)	intelligent	8
intéressant(m), intéressante(f)	interesting	5
jamais	never	15,16
jambon	ham	13
janvier(m)	January	7
jardin(m)	garden	5
jaune	yellow	5
je	I	13
jeudi(m)	Thursday	3

108

FRENCH WORD	ENGLISH	CHAPTER
joli(m), jolie(f)	pretty	15
jouer	to play	5
juillet(m)	July	7
juin(m)	June	7
jupe(f)	skirt	15
jusqu'à	until	6
l',le(m), la(f), les(pl)	the	3
là–bas	over there	15
lait (m)	milk	13
lentement	slowly	4
leur,leurs	their	8
libre	free	11
lit(m)	bed	1
livre(m)	book	11
loin	far	7
long(m), longue(f)	long	8
louer	to rent	16
loup(m)	wolf	13
lui	him	2
lundi(m)	Monday	5
lunettes(f pl)	glasses	8
madame(f)	Mrs.,madam	10
mademoiselle(f)	miss	10
magasin(m)	store	6
mai(m)	May	7
main(f)	hand	14
maintenant	now	10
mais	but	7
maison(f)	house	3
malade	sick	14
maman (f)	Mom, Mama	9
manger	to eat	1
manteau(m)	coat	15
maquillage (m)	make-up (comestics)	7
marcher	to walk	5
mardi(m)	Tuesday	5
mari(m)	husband	8
marié	married	8
marrant(m), marrante(f)	funny,humorous	5
marron	brown	7
mars(m)	March	7
matin(m)	morning	1
mauvais(m), mauvaise(f)	bad	9
même	same	15
merci	thank you	4
mercredi(m)	Wednesday	5
mère(f)	mother	7
mettre	to put(on)	15
midi(m)	noon	10
mieux	better	2,7
minuit(m)	midnight	10
moi	me	7
moins	less, minus	10
mois(m)	month	7
mon(m), ma(f), mes(pl)	my	8
monde(m)	world	7
monsieur(m)	sir	13
montagne(f)	mountain	7
monter	to go up	6
mot	word	7
musée d'art(m)	art museum	6
n'est-ce pas?	isn't it?, aren't you, etc	10
nager	to swim	13
ne...pas	not	10
neige (f)	snow	9
neuf	nine	2
neuvième	ninth	6
neveu(m)	nephew	8
nez(m)	nose	14
nièce(f)	niece	8
noir(m), noire(f)	black	5
nombre(m)	number	13
non	no	2
notre(f,m), nos	our	7
nous	we	1
nouveau(m), nouvelle(f)	new	12
novembre(m)	November	7
occupé	busy	5
octobre(m)	October	7
on	one, we	1,5
oncle(m)	uncle	7
onze	eleven	4

FRENCH WORD	ENGLISH	CHAPTER
orange	orange(color), fruit	5,13
où	where	1
ou	or	10
oui	yes	3
ouvert(m), ouverte(f)	open	6
ordinateur(m)	computer	11,16
pain(m)	bread	4
pantalon(m)	pants	15
par	by	16
par terre	on the ground	11
parce que	because	12
parler	to speak	1
partir	to leave	15
pâtes(f pl)	pasta	1
pauvre	poor	9
pendant	during	9
penser	to think	12
perdre	to lose	11
père(m)	father	5
personne(f)	person	11
petit déjeuner(m)	breakfast	1
petit(m),petite(f)	small	8
petite-fille(f)	granddaughter	8
petit-fils(m)	grandson	8
peu	little	12
peur	fear	14
peut-être	perhaps, maybe	7
pied(m)	foot	14
plage(f)	beach	1
pleuvoir	to rain	9
plus	more	6
pneu(m)	tire	16
poids(m)	weight	14
pomme(f)	apple	13
pont(m)	bridge	6
portable(m)	cellular phone	16
porter	to wear	15
poulet(m)	chicken	13
pour	in order to,for	6
pourquoi	why	13
pouvoir	to be able to	7
préférer	to prefer	6
premier(m), première(f)	first	1
prendre	to take	6
près de	near	2
présenter	to introduce	7
presque	almost	11
prêt	ready	15
printemps(m)	spring	7
prochain	next	9
professeur(m)	teacher	2
programmeur(m)	computer programmer	5
quai(m)	platform	10
quand	when	7
quatorze	fourteen	4
quatre	four	2
quatrième	fourth	6
que	that, what, which	10
quel(m), quelle(f)	what,which	7
quelque chose	something	13
qu'est-ce que	what	4
qui	who	9
quinze	fifteen	4
randonner	to hike	7
regarder	to look at	2
rendez-vous(m)	arrangement to meet	16
rendre visite à	to visit (someone)	9
renverser	to spill	16
répondre	to respond	7
rester	to stay	2
réunion(f)	meeting	15
robe(f)	dress	5
rose	pink	5
rouge	red	6
rue(f)	street	7
rhume(m)	cold (noun)	14
saison(f)	season	7
salle(f)	room	11
salut	hi	14
samedi(m)	Saturday	5
santé(f)	health	3
s'appeler	to be called	9

FRENCH WORD	ENGLISH	CHAPTER
s'asseoir	to sit down	11
sauf	except	14
saumon(m)	salmon	13
se promener	to go for a walk	6
se sentir	to feel	14
seize	sixteen	4
semaine(f)	week	5
sens(m)	meaning	14
sentir	to smell	11
sept	seven	2
septembre(m)	September	7
septième	seventh	6
s'il vous plaît, s'il te plaît	please	2
six	six	2
sixième	sixth	6
skier	to ski	7
soeur(f)	sister	8
soie(f)	silk	15
soif(f)	thirst	3
soir(m)	evening	10
soleil(m)	sunny	9
son(m), sa(f), ses(pl)	his, her	8
sortir	to leave, go out	2
sous	under	11
souvent	often	7
stylo(m)	pen	4
sur	on	11
surtout	especially	7
sympathique, sympa	nice	5
ton(m), ta(f), tes(pl)	your (familiar)	11
taille(f)	size	15
tant pis	nevermind	6
tante (f)	aunt	8
tapis(m)	rug, carpet	11
tarte(f)	pie	13
temps(m)	time, weather	9,10
tête(f)	head	14
thé	tea	13
timbre(f)	stamp	4
toujours	always	16
tourner	to turn	6
tous les deux	both	5
tout droit	straight ahead	6
tout le monde	everyone	7
tout(m), toute(f), tous(pl)	all	1
train(m)	train	5
travail(m)	work, job	6,9
travailler	to work	9
traverser	to cross	6
treize	thirteen	4
très	very	2
triste	sad	2
trois	three	2
troisième	third	6
trop	too	1
tu	you (informal)	7
un(m), une(f)	a, one	7
vacances(f pl)	vacation	7
valise(f)	suitcase	2
vélo(m)	bicycle	16
vendeur(m), vendeuse(f)	salesman, saleswoman	4
vendre	to sell	5
vendredi(m)	Friday	5
venir	to come	9
vent(m)	wind	9
ventre(m)	stomach	14
verre(m)	glass	10
vert	green	5
vêtements(m pl)	clothing	15
viande(f)	meat	1
vie(f)	life	16
vieux(m), vieille(f)	old	11
vin(m)	wine	13
vingt	twenty	3
visiter	to visit(a place)	6
voici	here is, here are	3
voilà	there is, there are	4
voir	to see	12
voiture(f)	car	1
voler	to steal, to fly	16
voleur(m)	thief	16
votre(m,f) vos (pl)	your	8

FRENCH WORD	ENGLISH	CHAPTER
voudrais	would like	1
vouloir	to want, wish	7
vous	you (formal)	3
voyage(m)	trip	7
voyager	to travel	7
vrai	true	6
vraiment	really	12
yeux(m pl)	eyes	5
zut	darn	10

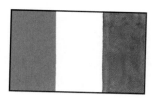

FRANCE

France, the largest country in western Europe, and the world's top tourist destination, has a long and a rich history with the United States:

- The Founding Fathers of the U.S. were all disciples of French philosophers like Montesquieu, Diderot, and Voltaire. Beginning in the early nineteenth century, an astonishingly large number of Americans (writers in particular) have found inspiration and acceptance in Paris by making it their temporary home. (Think Ernest Hemingway, John Steinbeck, Art Buchwald, Gertrude Stein, Janet Flanner, Henry James, Irwin Shaw, James Baldwin, W.H. Auden and many, many more.)

- The United States has been influenced by French architecture, food and wine, fashion, dance, film, arts, philosophy, and political thought. France embraces American culture through movies, music, books, TV and "franglais" (like *le parking, le fast food, le shopping, le marketing, le rock,* and *cool,* to name a few).

- The U.S. and France were allies during the War of 1812, the U.S. Civil War, and during both World Wars where fighting on French soil killed over a million French soldiers. To honor the friendship that was established between the two countries during the American Revolution, France presented the Statue of Liberty to the United States in 1886. It remains a symbol of not only freedom and democracy, but a reminder of the long-term friendship between the U.S. and France.

- Slightly smaller than Texas, France is amazingly diverse in its scenery and landscape. Beyond the large metropolitan areas like Paris, you will find rolling green hills, snow-capped mountains, and a sunny, Mediterranean coast. The super fast TGV trains leaving Paris make traveling around France quick and easy. Here are just a few areas you might want to visit:

1. <u>Normandy</u>: Mont-St- Michel; Bayeux tapestry; D-Day beaches; Camembert

2. <u>Alsace</u>: Strasbourg (where *pâté de foie gras* was invented); excellent food and wine; colorful festivals

3. <u>Loire Valley</u>: Magnificent castles (Chenonceaux, Chambord, Chinon); Vouvray wine

4. <u>Bordeaux (region)</u>: Atlantic beaches; La Rochelle; Futuroscope (a cinema theme park); Cognac; Bordeaux wines

5. <u>Provence</u>: Lavender fields, fascinating cities (Arles, Avignon, Marseille), outdoor markets, superb cuisine

OTHER FRENCH SPEAKING COUNTRIES

French is spoken on five continents and is the first or second language in close to 50 countries. Some local dialects exist, but knowing your fundamental French will help you have a rewarding experience in francophone countries as you get to know the people who live there. Here are only some of the places you may be able to practice your French someday if you travel there.

BELGIUM
la Belgique

- Flemish speak Dutch; Walloons speak French; many people speak English
- Bruges– "Venice of the North" because of its canals; medieval architecture
- Known for its mussels, chocolate, beer, lace and warm hospitality

SWITZERLAND
la Suisse

- French is one of four national languages (along with German, Italian, and Romansh)
- Seventy percent of country covered by the Alps
- Frequent trains that take you through spectacular scenery run all over (even up steep inclines)
- Discover the "Swiss Riviera" along Lake Geneva: Montreaux, Vevey, Lausanne and Geneva
- Sample Swiss culinary specialties like raclette and fondue

TAHITI
le Tahiti

- One of 120 islands of the French Polynesia archipelago in the Pacific Ocean
- Tropical paradise and close to islands of Moorea, Bora Bora, and others
- Smoked breadfruit, banana groves, gorgeous flowers, waterfalls, Gaughin Museum

SENEGAL
le Sénégal

- Dakar, port city and capital, has open-air markets, outdoor cafes, many art galleries and studios
- Peaceful and beautiful Island of Gorée was once center of slave trade. Visit the preserved "Slave House"
- 350 miles of beaches - go south of Dakar for best locations
- "Pink Lake" shallow, warm, and completely pink. Everything floats on it because of its high salinity.

PARIS MONUMENTS AND MUSEUMS

The Eiffel Tower, built in 1889, is of course the most well-known of Paris monuments and one that is very impressive close up as well as far away. It is about 1,000 feet tall, contains nearly 7,000 tons of metal and has three levels, accessible by elevators or by climbing the 1,665 steps. Be sure to catch a glimpse of *la tour Eiffel (eh-fel)* at night when it is illuminated.

The Arc de Triomphe, the largest triumphal arch in the world, is a massive monument that was built by Napoleon I to commemorate his victories. Located at the western end of the famous Champs-Elysées *(shaN-zay-lee-zay)*, there are 12 avenues (the Place d'Etoile – the "star") that radiate from the arc. The bustling traffic moves in a circular pattern, which is viewable from the observation deck at the top of the arc (where you also get a panoramic view of the Champs-Elysées as well as other Paris landmarks).

Known for its gargoyles and the Hunchback, Notre Dame Cathedral *(nohtr dahm)* is a masterpiece of Gothic architecture, constructed during the 12th and 13th centuries. It is located in the center of Paris on the "Ile de la Cité", the island in the River Seine *(sehn)*. Climb to the top for a bird's eye view of the city or admire it from the river when you take a "Bateau-Mouche" tour down the Seine.

A visit to Paris would not be complete without viewing at least some of the art in the largest museum in the western world, the Louvre. One of the entrances to the Louvre is through the glass pyramid built by the American architect, I.M.Pei. To view Europe's greatest collection of Impressionist art, go to the Orsay Museum (Musée d'Orsay), across the river from the Louvre. Don't miss the Pompidou Center for a chance to see an incredible collection of modern art.

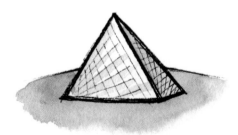

Nearly 100 museums in and around Paris allow you many exciting choices, whether your interests are fashion, wine, technology, sculpture, stamps, dolls, photography, music, or just about anything. Take advantage of special exhibits that may be open during your visit. Other places to include on your itinerary: Versailles (just outside of Paris), the grand palace of the kings, Père Lachaise Cemetery, where you can find the graves of famous French citizens as well as American rocker, Jim Morrison, and the Grande Arche de la Défense, the enormous Twentieth Century complex in the suburb of La Défense that is in sharp contrast to the historical significance of the Arc de Triomphe.

QUEBEC

Three times the size of France, Québec, *"La Belle Province"*, is Canada's largest province. About half of the population of *Québec* (kay-behk) lives in *Montréal* (mohN-ray-al), a festive city known for its night life and variety of restaurants. Most of the other "Quebecers" or *Québecois* (kay-bay-kwa) live in the other cities and towns along the St. Lawrence river, including Québec City, the provincial capital and magical city that feels like you are in Europe with its cobblestone streets and historical significance. The scenery is spectacular in Québec. There are close to a million lakes, over one hundred thousand rivers, and about half the land is forested. It is known for very cold, snowy winters, but it has four distinct seasons, and tourists visit at all times of year.

French is the official language of Québec. *Québécois* is the name of the language as well as the people. The vast majority of the people are *francophones* (French speaking). In fact, Montréal has more French speakers than any other city in the world besides Paris. Many of the 10% who call themselves "anglophones" are also bilingual. Most of the anglophones live in the Montreal area so you will hear English spoken there (and to a lesser extent in Québec City), but you will not find English on road signs, maps, or brochures. It helps to become familiar with *Québécois*. It will sound different from "France" French not only in the differences in pronunciation, but in the many unique words and expressions. Here is a partial list of words and expressions that will help you:

Québécois	French	English
la fin de semaine	le week-end	weekend
arrêt	le stop	stop
le stationnement	le parking	parking
magasiner	shopper	to shop
le déjeuner	le petit déjeuner	breakfast
le dîner	le déjeuner	lunch
le souper	le dîner	dinner
un dépanneur	un petit magasin	a convenience store
une broue	une bière	a beer
une patate frite	des frites	French fries
une tabagie	un tabac	cigarette stand
courriel	email	email
un char	une voiture	a car
mon chum	mon ami, mon copain	my friend/buddy
une vue	un film	a movie
des flots	des enfants	children
des barniques	des lunettes	eyeglasses
un pitou	un chien	a dog
un minou	un chat	a cat
il fait frette	il fait très froid	it's very cold
il mouille	il pleut	it's raining
sacrer son camp	partir/quitter	to leave
Pantoute!	Pas du tout!	Not at all!

Paste these removable stickers around your work and home.
It will re-enforce what you've learned!

(zhuh mah-pehl)
Je m'appelle...

(kohN-mahN voo zah-play voo)
Comment vous appelez–vous?

(sa meh tay-gahl)
Ça m'est égal.

(sah vah)
Ça va?

(zhuh pahr luhN puh frahN-seh)
Je parle un peu français.

(zhuh nseh pah)
Je ne sais pas.

(ohN nyee vah)
On y va!

(bohN ah-pay-tee)
Bon appétit

(BohN koo-rahzh)
Bon courage!

(seh lah vee)
C'est la vie!

(seel voo pleh)
s'il vous plaît

(duh ryaN)
De rien.

(mwa-o-see)
Moi aussi.

(dah-kohr)
D'accord.

(zhay fahN)
J'ai faim.

(zhay swahf)
J'ai soif.

(seh zhay-nyahl)
C'est génial.

(suh neh pah grahv)
Ce n'est pas grave.

(vwa-see)
Voici.

(kehl shahNs)
Quelle chance!

(doo vuh-nay voo)
D'où venez–vous?

(kohN-byaN sa koot)
Combien ça coûte?

(byaN sewr)
Bien sûr!

(eel feh sho)
Il fait chaud.

(tahN pee)
Tant pis!

(seh vreh)
C'est vrai.

(ah byaN-to)
A bientôt!

(ah too tah luhr)
à tout à l'heure

(toot sweet)
tout de suite

(kohN-pruh-nay voo)
Comprenez–vous?

(duh tahN zahN tahN)
de temps en temps

(zhuh voo-dreh)
Je voudrais …

(oo eh)
Où est-ce....?

(keh-skee lya)
Qu'est–ce qu'il y a?

(zhuh muh sahN mahl)
Je me sens mal.

(zhuh swee fah-tee-gay)
Je suis fatigué.

(kehl bohnee-day)
Quelle bonne idée!

(sa mahrsh)
Ça marche.

(zhuh mahN veh)
Je m'en vais.

(o-ruh-vwahr)
Au revoir.